THE BOOK OF ACTS IN HISTORY

THE BOOK OF ACTS
IN HISTORY

BY

HENRY J. CADBURY

D.D., GLASGOW

HOLLIS PROFESSOR OF DIVINITY EMERITUS
HARVARD UNIVERSITY

HARPER & BROTHERS PUBLISHERS

New York

PREFACE

A popular fictitious Christian book of perhaps the fourth century, named the *Apocalypse of Paul,* tells this story of its discovery. A pious man living at Tarsus in the house that had been St. Paul's was directed by an angel to dig into the foundation and there, in a marble box sealed with lead, he found the book itself and also the shoes of Paul 'wherein he walked when he taught the word of God'. In a similar way the contemporary English historian, Arthur Bryant, has written of his *Discovering That the Past Was Real* by studying a whole batch of documents from a single family in Cheshire over a period of three centuries.

Something like these two experiences comes to one who undertakes to put the Acts of the Apostles back into the context of its times. We may not find an apostle's actual shoes, but we can walk where he walked, see and feel as he did and become increasingly at home in the apostolic age and world. In many respects that world is alien to the ordinary Bible reader, inwardly and outwardly. Like our own cosmopolitan world it was the fusion of several cultures, oriental, Greek, Roman, Jewish and Christian; but all of those cultures are now nineteen centuries behind us. Even the Judaism and the Christianity of that day differed widely from their modern successors.

Except scholars who specialize in the ancient cultures few readers of the Book of Acts recognize how well it fits its contemporary setting. There is a natural gulf between the past and the present, and in addition the special treatment accorded for many generations to the Bible has tended to isolate it quite as much as to honour it. The unnatural attitude to it often thus engendered in both the pious and the indifferent has taken from the Book of Acts its impression of throbbing lifelikeness.

The purpose of these pages is to establish not so much the accuracy of the book as the realism of the scenes and customs and mentality which it reflects. More than most parts of the Bible this unique narrative of Christian beginnings lends itself to such treatment.

For over twenty years the two-volume work which I have

called *Luke-Acts* was the centre of my study and writing, ending with the Commentary and Additional Notes on the Acts of the Apostles which Professor Kirsopp Lake and I published in 1933. Since that time new questions and answers about that volume have spontaneously come to my attention, beginning with my travelling that same year for the first time to the Near East. When therefore I was invited twenty years later to give a series of Lowell Lectures in Boston in 1953 sufficient material had accumulated and I wrote out for that purpose the six chapters which follow. Some of the material was used previously for the Aytoun Lectures at the Selly Oak Colleges, England, or the Carew Lectures at Hartford Seminary, and some of it afterwards for the Jackson Lectures at the Perkins School of Theology of Southern Methodist University at Dallas.

This book is therefore less a repetition than epilegomena to my earlier studies, and is retained in the form intelligible to the ordinary reader which lectures require. Five chapters deal respectively with the five concentric cultural environments already mentioned. The sixth chapter, with the same eye for the natural contemporary situation, attempts to reconstruct the early history of the book *after* it was written just as my *Making of Luke-Acts* tried to reconstruct the prior historical process of composition.

For the sake of those interested in pursuing the evidence further some notes have been added (but not indexed). The notes are admittedly somewhat sporadic and not exhaustive, intended often to call attention to more recent or less familiar literature. There is no reason to suppose that either new angles of approach to Acts or useful literature about it will not continue to accumulate.

Grateful acknowledgment is hereby made to several of my former colleagues who 'at sundry times and in divers manners' have contributed to this book with their good judgment and learning. They will perhaps recognize their suggestions. I do not name them except one, using this opportunity to pay special tribute to the encouragement, inspiration and friendship of the late Willard L. Sperry, Dean of the Harvard Divinity School.

PENDLE HILL   HENRY J. CADBURY
WALLINGFORD, PENNA.

CONTENTS

THE BOOK OF ACTS IN HISTORY

CHAPTER I

GENERAL

The title of these chapters would have been less ambiguous if, instead of writing on the Book of Acts in History, I had chosen to write on the history in the Book of Acts. Perhaps the subject would also have proved more attractive to readers. There can be no doubt that this earliest little essay of Church History is one of the most interesting and important narratives ever written. Its importance is shown by the extraordinary darkness which comes over us as students of history when rather abruptly this guide leaves us with Paul a prisoner in Rome. The story of the early church becomes a conjectural haze at this point, a congeries of disconnected data which neither the apocryphal legends of the later centuries nor the scholarly guesses of recent years can form into a continuous pattern. As with a certain character in the book itself (13: 11) immediately mist and darkness fall upon us and we are left blind seeking, as we go about, someone to lead us by the hand. For a whole generation of history or, if we include the Gospel, for two generations the anonymous writer to Theophilus, whom from convention if not from conviction we may call Luke,[1] has supplied a continuous account of the Christian movement as he promised in his preface. Whether he intended a third volume and, if so, whether he wrote it we do not know. In any case we do not have it, and the lack of it makes us the more appreciative of what we have. 'You never miss the water till the well runs dry.'

The historical worth of the Acts of the Apostles is not to be expressed merely in such negative terms. In itself it often carries its own evidences of accuracy, of intelligent grasp of its theme, of fullness of information. Its stories are not thin and colourless but packed with variety and substance. There is reason for the modern reader to ponder them carefully, to examine them in detail and to compare them point for point throughout the volume. To retell that story after the author would be a valuable and worth while exercise. It is constantly being so retold and each generation that has done so has found much of interest in the process.

For my own part, however, I have for a number of years found more intriguing the study of the relation of the Book of Acts to its wider contemporary environment. Not the history that it relates but its own place in history is the subject which I hope to illustrate in these chapters. The two topics cannot be separated. The data which throw light on the history in Acts are also the data which confirm its place in history. But there is a difference in the approach. To a large extent the material with which I shall deal is capable of an apologetic use. It can be cited to show that the author of Acts is dealing with fact and reality.[2] Whenever a monument or ancient writing attests a circumstance that appears in the volume of scripture it can be seized upon as confirming the reliability of the latter in general as well as in the particular instance.

I am willing to acknowledge the legitimacy and interest of this process when it is not overdone. I understand why it is the natural approach for so many minds, but it is not my present approach. It seeks to add to the authority of the sacred volume the confirmation of secular evidence. My interest is rather to place the book in its historical setting. For really more important than any exact correspondence of its narrative with historical fact is the general fitness to its time. Even though the author interprets natural events supernaturally and recites speeches which were never exactly so delivered, he interpreted those events much as the actors and eyewitnesses did and perhaps he knew better than we moderns would what the actors were likely to feel and say under the circumstances.

There may seem to be something rather futile in this undertaking. Here is a book written in the first century of our era about events of the same period. Can we not take for granted without proof that in both its manner and its contents it will fit that time and the places of which it speaks? Is there not something presumptuous in confirming its local and contemporary colour? Should we be justified in doubting any statement or detail because we happened not to have independent confirmation? But when we have confirmation is that especially surprising? Take for example the story of the riot at Ephesus in Acts 19. We are told that it was instigated by a maker of silver shrines of Artemis and that it took place in the theatre. Now we can prove by countless references that the theatres of ancient cities were a usual place for formal and informal civic gatherings. The site of the theatre at Ephesus is known and some sculptured panels from its stage can be seen in the Kunsthistorisches Museum at Vienna. We even have references in inscriptions to political gatherings in the theatre at Ephesus. On the other hand though other forms of memento or souvenir of the Ephesian Artemis are known, silver replicas of her image, and terra-cotta models of her temple, and though she and her temple were known throughout the world as one of its seven wonders, there is to date I believe no evidence that it was customary to make silver images of her Ephesian temple. Metal replicas of other temples or shrines have been found, but not of this one.

There is the possibility of a mistake here. As we wrote some years ago:

E. L. Hicks, editor of the corpus of Ephesian inscriptions, pointed out that 'Shrine-maker' was the official title of a board of wardens or vestry of the temple of Artemis at Ephesus. There appear to have been twelve, two each for the six tribes. In the Expositor i. (1890), pp. 401 ff., he made the brilliant suggestion that Demetrius was a silversmith, who was also 'Shrine-maker', and that Luke's phrase, 'making shrines' is a misunderstanding of his title. Presumably his interest in the cult of Artemis was that he made silver statuettes of Artemis of a kind familiar to archaeologists. Hicks went further and identified him with a Demetrius who is mentioned as a 'Shrine-maker' in Brit. Mus. Ins. iii. 2, 578. His first suggestion seems extremely probable, as even supposing that this part of Acts is the first-hand observation of an eyewitness, he is quite likely to have misunderstood such a curious phrase as 'Shrine-maker' = 'vestryman' when it obviously ought to mean 'maker of a temple'. Official titles are very easy to misinterpret. For instance, comparatively few foreigners understand what is meant in English when an eminent judge is described as 'an Elder Brother of the Trinity'.[3]

What now shall we make of this situation? Shall we have doubt about the unconfirmed item while we accept the confirmed ones? And if not, is there any real value in showing that sporadically we happen to have evidence from other sources for a story that no one expects to be generally fictitious anyhow? Finding the evidence and applying it to the case which it fits is a lot of fun. It even goes under the name of scholarship. But if you don't find it, is it not all the same? It is very exciting when my friend Professor Hotson discovers in the Public Record Office who killed Kit Marlowe or with whom Shakespeare's father had a lawsuit. But after all what difference does it make? The unknown history must somehow have fitted what we know even if we never discover it. Marlowe died somehow and if he was murdered somebody must have killed him. Shakespeare's father must have had some kind of dealings with his contemporaries— and if sometimes they were law suits, well why should they not be?

Now a scholar, as my most intimate critics tell me, is largely a cross between a detective and a puzzle addict. Perhaps that is the reason why so many of my professional colleagues read and some of them even write detective stories.[4] And as for puzzles, there is not much difference between fitting the data of the Book of Acts into their contemporary setting and fitting queer-shaped pieces of wood back into the coloured picture from which a jig-saw has cut them or of rearranging crosswise and downwards far-fetched words which some ingenious person has taken out of a dictionary and arranged in advance in a complicated acrostic. In the case of history there is this difference that accident and the mere lapse of time and not the intentional maker of puzzles have scattered the pieces and even lost many of them or obscured the original pattern.

The task set before us has more importance than mere amusement. Nor is it only to confirm the accuracy of Acts that one does well to consider its relation to the ancient world. There is too much tendency to regard Christianity as something unique and apart in its origin. Yet it did not grow up *in vacuo*. It bore close likeness to the world which surrounded it. They were typical first century minds that gave form to its thought, as they were first century cities that gave it geographical setting. Even much of its religion was in accord not merely with Jewish but even with pagan outlook. If we are to distinguish in historic Christianity either the primitive or the original elements we must recognize what is simply common in antiquity. Much that may seem to us distinctive is merely unmodern or unwestern. There is parabolic meaning which the author of Acts did not intend in the statement that on the day of Pentecost the widely representative group which was gathered in Jerusalem heard Christianity presented in the languages in which they were born. In spite of their linguistic and cultural variation the primitive Christian message was perhaps more congenial to their minds than to ours.

The setting of the New Testament in its contemporary environment should correct also the tendency unduly to modernize it. I have had occasion elsewhere to criticize our modernizing of the Gospels.[5] I suppose we do much the same with Acts, though less conspicuously. It is useful to try to put Peter and Paul not in our world but into the ancient world of their own with which casual readers of Acts are really little acquainted.

The material available for our purpose is quite varied. We wish to show the fitness of details in Acts to our other knowledge of its environment. For this purpose all that we can learn from outside sources about the persons and places and events which it mentions will be of use. But beside this exact correspondence we may add more general agreements. For some of these I think we need to coin the phrase 'contemporary colour' —a phrase analogous to the more familiar 'local colour'. The author's own language, his literary form, his point of view toward his material, are part of this, and then in his story the customs or actions recounted may tally strikingly with what we know of the environment or the age. Perhaps the personal names are a form of contemporary colour which one does not always think of in this way. Yet those in Acts, representing as they do several cultural groups,[6] are themselves of interest in relation to contemporary practice among the Jews, among other Semites, among Greeks and Romans. One could devote a whole chapter to these alone. They will be briefly mentioned in each succeeding chapter.

The sources from which our illustrative material comes are also varied. The contemporary writers are one source, not merely the Greek and Latin historians and geographers but writers in many other fields as well. Especially intimate of course are the writings of Josephus and the letters of Paul. The dovetailing of these into the narrative of Acts is a puzzle familiar to scholars and very similar to the puzzles already mentioned. It is astonishing how out of the way writers sometimes give insight into the Book of Acts. I have used for this purpose naturalists, astrologers,[7] horse-doctors,[8] magicians, tacticians, rhetoricians, as well as authors of belles-lettres. Sometimes the fictitious romances offer the best parallel. I do not know where one can get so many illustrations of the idiom and ideas of the author of Acts in 150 pages as in the love story of his near contemporary, Chariton of Aphrodisias.

The Greek papyri are another source of New Testament illustration. Their novelty in this field, their assured genuineness even to the spelling, and their unartificial popular character make them especially interesting. They may be used for many linguistic details of Acts though these are difficult to illustrate in English writing.

The papyri also give suggestive parallels to incidents of ordinary life. Recall the tragic episode when Paul stopped off for a week at Troas:

> And on the first day of the week when we were gathered together to break bread Paul addressed them, as he was going to leave the next day, and he prolonged his discourse until midnight. And there were many lamps in the upper room where we were gathered. And a lad named Eutychus, sitting by the window, beginning to be overcome by deep sleep, fell from the third floor to the bottom and

was taken up dead. But Paul went down and leaned over him, and embracing him said, 'Do not make a fuss, for his life is in him' . . . And they brought away the boy alive and were immensely comforted. (Acts 20: 7-12.)

Compare with that this official order for a coroner's inquest, dated to the day and month A.D. 182 and enclosing the request from a 'next of kin'.[9] I quote only the latter.

> To Hierax, strategus, from Leonides, also called Serenus, whose mother is stated to be Tauris, of Senepta. At a late hour yesterday the 6th, while a festival was taking place at Senepta and the clapper players were giving their usual performance at the house of Plution my son in law . . . his slave Epaphroditus, aged about 8 years, wishing to lean out over the roof (?) of the said house and watch the clapper players, fell and was killed. I therefore present this application and ask you, if it please you, to appoint one of your assistants to come to Senepta in order that the body of Epaphroditus may receive proper laying out and burial.

> The 23rd year of emperor Claudius Marcus
> Aurelius Commodus Antoninus Augustus
> Armenian Median Parthian Sarmatian
> German Maximus   Athur 7

Unfortunately Epaphroditus at Senepta had not like Eutychus at Troas—whose very name means lucky—a wonder-worker to bring him to life. We may compare rather an inscription about another mishap in the fourth century B.C. at Epidaurus in Greece at the shrine of Aesculapius, the god of healing.

> When the suppliants were already asleep in the temple, Aeschines climbing a tree peered over into the sacred yard. So falling down from the tree on the pickets of the fence he spiked his eyes. But being in a sorry plight and having become blind he supplicated the god and slept in the temple and became well.[10]

Other contemporary sources are inscriptions and coins. These have perhaps not been used as much in recent years as have the papyri by New Testament scholars. I suspect even the coins have still some interesting data to give us respecting questions of chronology.[11] For example, no date would be more useful or the chronology of Paul and none more natural to expect to find than the year in which Felix the Roman procurator of Judea was succeeded by Porcius Festus—for which event historians can set a date with no certainty between 55 and 60. Now it has been pointed out that a new Judean coinage begins in the fifth year of Nero, that is before October A.D. 59. Is it not probable that it is due to the arrival of a new procurator?

The illustrative sources need not be entirely contemporary just as they need not be entirely local. For the military life of the first century Roman Empire one can use inscriptions in Britain and Spain and Austria and Egypt to illustrate what Acts relates in Palestine. So also for oriental life in the first century one can often find the best illustrations from other times. That is what we mean by the unchanging East. A few years ago in trying to discover what is meant in Acts 27 : 17 by 'undergirding' the ship I found one interpretation was best illustrated graphically not by any contemporary Roman evidence but by an Egyptian drawing of an expedition of Queen Hatseput to the land of Punt some eighteen and a half centuries earlier. The drawing is not unknown to students of the Egypt of that early time. But it may be worth while to know that the most available reproduction of the drawing and its details of undergirding is the special series of Egyptian postage stamps issued for the International Congress of Navigation at Cairo in 1926, eighteen and a half centuries after the date in Acts.[12]

In dealing with this varied material several methods are possible. One could go through the Book of Acts in order and pick out illustrations from whatever source they come, following the sequence of the narrative. Or one could divide the illustrations according to the source from which they are derived dealing separately with evidence from coins, evidence from inscriptions, evidence from each of several classes of ancient writers. But instead of these methods I think I shall rather divide my illustrations according to the cultural group or field to which they belong. In doing so I shall be reminding us of an essential fact about the background of Acts and that is its multiple strands. Four main elements stand out: the Roman, the Hellenistic, the Jewish and the Christian and to each of these one of the succeeding chapters will be devoted.

Of course the interesting thing about these factors is that they overlap each other so fully. They were not water-tight compartments in any sense. They are rather strands that one can see interwoven in the story of Acts—first one and then another appearing. Take the figure of the Apostle Paul. Within the equivalent of a single chapter the author makes it clear that he is a Roman citizen, and born one too (22 : 27-28), that he is no barbarian but can speak Greek (21 : 37-38), that he was reared in the strict law of Judaism (22 : 3), and that he has been directly called by Christ to preach his name to the Gentiles (22 : 21). He has the proud consciousness of belonging to the most genuine character of each of our four strands.

But even these four strands do not by any means exhaust the cultural background of Acts. They are each of them an élite or, if you prefer the spelling, an elect group contrasted to a wider circle. The ordinary denizen of the Eastern Empire was no *civis Romanus* like Paul but a *peregrinus* or unnaturalized subject. Though Greek culture and language had made considerable impress on this same area there were still the millions of people whom the Greek must regard as barbarians. For the Jews a similar contrasting term was the Gentiles, while of course the Christians, a few hundred or at most a few thousands, though but lately gathered out of many tongues and peoples, Jew, Gentile, barbarian, Scythian, bond or free, had as Christians a basis of unity that marked them off as self-consciously from those who did not believe as though they were an entirely different culture. For the major parts of the Empire the Christians came to be regarded as a kind of third race.[13]

For these elements in the background of Acts no single name is obvious, since the opposites which we have spoken of,—*peregrini*, barbarians, Gentiles, non-believers—are not appropriate. From our modern viewpoint this other, fifth element is often called oriental. But so is Judaism. Like Judaism much of the fifth strand is Semitic. Without giving it a name we may devote the remainder of this chapter to some illustrations of this aspect of the background of Acts.

In concentrating on the oriental, or indeed on any of the cultural strands in Acts, one ought not to forget how closely they are interwoven. Homogeneity was not characteristic of population in the Roman empire, even locally. Mixing occurred—in the army, through trade and migration, by the process of slavery, and in other ways. There was juxtaposition of variant groups, not merely upon local frontiers. Ancient writers were especially impressed with this feature in the city of Rome. To a less extent it was characteristic of other cities, like Antioch on the Orontes, Seleucia on the Tigris and Alexandria on the Nile and probably in other or smaller cities among the so-called 'cities of St. Paul'. Modern writers have discussed race mixture in the Roman Empire more in connection with slavery.[14] The data available here is abundant and incidental and shows individuals of very different strands occupying places close together. There is however a whole series of other factors which turned the Empire into a melting pot, and had its effect for better or for worse on its subsequent history.[15] I am not speaking merely of race mixture by marriage. That took place. Acts itself introduces us—and that in a smallish inland town (Acts 16: 1)—to Timothy whose mother was a Jewess and his father 'a Greek'. Even this word Greek probably conceals racial varieties. In the New Testament it is sometimes nearly if not quite the same as Gentile. Hellenic stock in the narrower sense can no more be assumed by the word Greek than it can from a person's use of Greek language or his bearing of a Greek name. A woman living in the Levant and described in the Gospels as Syro-phoenician or Canaanite is called also Greek.[16] In fact she would belong precisely to the extra or fifth category to which we have referred.

The extraneous factor in Acts that we are dealing with appears in the ancient world in more than one form. On the outskirts of the Empire and scarcely touched by Greek or Roman influences, old indigenous civilizations survived. Even in the heart of the Empire and in lands long conquered politically and culturally by the West, indigenous forms of life, speech and thought still pre-

vailed, partly overlaid by Greco-Roman life and partly parallel
to it. Finally the cosmopolitan life of the age, the abundance of
travel, the curiosity about alien cultures and religions, led at this
time to fresh transfers of oriental blood and culture into the
West. For all these three forms the Book of Acts provides hints
or illustrations. Referring to the last of them Juvenal, the
Roman satirist, complained that the Orontes emptied into the
Tiber.[17] Could we have a more exact illustration of his complaint
than Luke's story of Paul's propaganda among the Gentiles
beginning precisely at Syrian Antioch on the Orontes and ending at Rome on the Tiber? It was another Roman writer, Sal-
lust, who, changing the metaphor a little, referred explicitly to
Christianity as illustrating the tendency of all evil to congregate
at Rome as in a cesspool.[18] And a third Roman writer, Suetonius, agrees with the author of Acts (18 : 2) in telling us that the
emperor Claudius came to regard the Jews as so pernicious as to
adopt the tactics of a certain dictator of our own time and deliberately expelled them from Rome.[19] There are other hints
in Acts of an anti-Semitism which we know from other sources
existed in the first century. Was it anything else which led the
people of Corinth to beat Sosthenes the ruler of the synagogue
before the very judgment seat of Gallio (18 : 17)? It was certainly
not because they loved Paul the more, though the Christian
historian can draw his own satisfaction out of the unexpected
way in which the tables were turned. And was not Alexander
in the theatre at Ephesus again a near victim of a pogrom, though
again the author does not make quite clear the situation as he
writes; 'And at the instigation of the Jews some of the crowd put
forward Alexander, and Alexander motioned with his hand and
wished to make a defence to the people. But when they recognized that he was a Jew there was a single cry from them all,
howling for about two hours, "Great is Artemis of the Ephesians,
great is Artemis of the Ephesians"' (19 : 33-34). That slogan, so
characteristic of ancient acclamation, would strike terror into the
heart of any Jew.

These episodes have to do with Jews and Christians. With
Semites or Orientals in the wider sense the Book of Acts has

some interesting contacts. Such persons often lie close under the surface not only of Jewish and Christian religion but also of Greek culture. They might speak Greek and carry even Greek names. I think, however, the author of Acts was sensitive about both non-Greek names and non-Greek language.[20] He had himself the viewpoint of a Hellene and as a man of letters he was likely to apologize for non-Hellenic names and to use them sparingly.[21]

Indeed with all this oriental matter the Book of Acts gives us a double outlook—the actual oriental elements as they existed in the ancient scene, and (what is fully as interesting) the reaction of the author himself to the barbarian data in his story. 'The glance of the author', writes Harnack of Acts, 'surveys the greater part of the known world from the Parthians and Medes to Rome, and from the Ethiopians to Bithynia.'[22] If the word had not recently been pre-empted for use in a special sense the English 'ecumenical' might have been adopted to name the world-wide intercultural features of antiquity reflected in the Book of Acts. Four times he refers in his book to the whole οἰκουμένη or *orbis terrarum*—what we should call the 'known world', and I think on one occasion (2 : 9-11) he essays pretty much to fill in its parts with a list of names. In many ways his was already 'one world'.

The story of Pentecost is certainly testimony to his outlook on a very polyglot world. This is the more the case, if, as many scholars believe, he has really altered the ecstatic phenomena of early Christian worship as described by Paul (1 Cor. 12-14) into a philological miracle. While we cannot be sure whether the company in Jerusalem were born Jews or adherents to Judaism or in the main completely Gentile, it is evident that the author thinks of them as representing over a dozen different native languages and as hearing the gospel each in their own language in which they were born: 'Parthians and Medes and Elamites and dwellers in Mesopotamia, Judea and Cappadocia, Pontus and Asia, Phrygia and Pamphylia, Egypt and the parts of Libya which is near Cyrene, and the residents, Roman citizens and Jews and proselytes, Cretans and Arabians' (2 : 9-11).

As a matter of fact such a variety of countries might easily be represented in Jerusalem on a feast day, though it is doubtful whether they could not communicate in a much smaller number of languages. Bilingualism was very prevalent in the ancient world and with no miracle they could mostly have talked to each other in Greek. Furthermore, the list does not seem to represent a careful linguistic or ethnographic mapping.[23] Even if the story is not to be accepted as exact history, it does offer us at the beginning a reminder of the cultural amalgam of the scenes in which the book moves and shows to us an author who as the historian of early Christianity is impressed with its catholic character and mission. He may not carry out the variety of this programmatic frontispiece, but we shall note carefully in the later chapters of his work those scenes where, whether intentionally or not, he brings us into contact with these less familiar strands of his world. The following is one of those scenes:

> But an angel of the Lord spoke to Philip, saying, Rise and go southwards on the road which goes down from Jerusalem to Gaza. (This is deserted.) And he arose and went, and behold an Ethiopian man, a eunuch, minister of Candace, queen of the Ethiopians, who was in charge of all her treasure, who had come on a pilgrimage to Jerusalem, and was returning and was seated in his coach and reading the prophet Isaiah. And the Spirit said to Philip, 'Go and join this coach.' And Philip ran up and heard him reading Isaiah the prophet, and said, 'Do you after all understand what you are reading?' (8 : 26-30)

This story, including the sequel which I have not quoted, is familiar, and it has a romantic character that neither the author nor his first readers would have missed. To Homer and to Isaiah the Ethiopians doubtless represented a geographical extreme, and one is tempted to suppose that our author included the story to illustrate the fulfilment of the promise with which this book begins of witnessing under the power of the Spirit in Jerusalem, in all Judea and Samaria, and to the end of the earth (1 : 8). Philip, who has just been to Samaria, does not go to Ethiopia; instead, as with the nationals represented at Pentecost, an Ethiopian has come to Jerusalem and Philip intercepts him before he has gone far on his way home. Whether the author of Acts, like later tradition, thought of the Ethiopian as later converting his fellow countrymen we cannot say. The present emperor of the little kingdom and its indigenous and independent Christianity trace their origin to a later time. And there are students of Acts who claim that this Ethiopian and not the centurion Cornelius is the first Gentile Christian. Luke does not tell and we cannot be sure that he was a Gentile at all. His visit to Jerusalem and his reading of the Jewish prophet suggest that if not a Jew he was at least one of that very large group of persons half converted to the worship of Yahweh. Nor does Luke think of him as a foreigner in speech. Philip converses with him without either interpreter or miracle of tongues. Nor are we to suppose that the roll of Isaiah which he read was yet translated into what we call Ethiopic but that it was in the same Greek from which Luke quotes a selected passage, in its form so strikingly different from the Hebrew.[24]

And yet, if the story is true, it brings us into contact with a peculiar and exotic country. It was not our modern Ethiopia or Abyssinia but part of what we call Anglo-Egyptian Sudan along the Nile—the so-called kingdom of Meroe. It was not subject to the Romans though in 23 B.C. a punitive expedition of Roman soldiers under the prefect Gaius Petronius invaded and defeated the Ethiopians. The Greek geographer Strabo who tells the story speaks of the queen of the Ethiopians at that time (and his own) as Candace, a masculine woman, who was blind in one eye. The agreement of the name with Acts is interesting but the dates are too far apart to be the same person. Only slightly nearer in date is the queen of Ethiopia under Nero, whom Pliny the Elder mentions.[25]. She also was named Candace. Later Greek writers seem to conclude that queens ruled in Ethiopia more than kings and that their name was always Candace. According to Bion of Soli, who, perhaps in the second century B.C., wrote a work on Ethiopia, the title was given to the queen mother who was the real head of the government. Her husband was unimportant, for the king, her son, was counted as the child of the Sun.[26] Possibly some such lore as this was already in circulation when Luke wrote, and his story may be derived from and intended for a circle which had a curiosity and a body of legend about this remotest of lands. Perhaps the queen who had dared match herself with the legions of Augustus lingered on in history. It would not be the only instance in which Luke has been accused of applying a local official's name to a much later date.

There are other aspects of the story which also fit the Hellenic viewpoint. That the queen's officer was a eunuch suits also the reports of barbarian civilization cherished by the Greeks. Already Herodotus[27] reports that among the barbarians eunuchs are especially prized as servants because of their trustworthiness, while Plutarch explains that Lysimachus resented being called treasurer by his rival Demetrius because eunuchs were then usually selected for treasurers. Indeed the very word chosen for the anonymous official's rank by Luke—δυνάστης—has perhaps something of the oriental sound to ancient ears that pundit or vizier might have in our time. In Jeremiah 34 : 19 it is the Greek translation for the Aramaic *saris*, which itself is often used rather of an officer than of an actual eunuch.

If, however, we are to compare Luke's story not merely with the viewpoint to Ethiopia of other Mediterranean men of letters but with native evidence we run into difficulties or at least obscurities. The history and language of the ancient Ethiopians are imperfectly known. In spite of the valiant efforts of Professor Griffith its inscriptions are still only half understood. Whatever language a treasurer travelling from Jerusalem might read in his copy of Isaiah he did not read Greek on the pyramids of his kings and queens at home. These are inscribed 'sometimes in hieroglyphics which appeared to imitate approximately the Egyptian hieroglyphics and sometimes in a cursive script unlike anything hitherto known'. The whole civilization indeed is unhellenic and dominantly or decayedly Egyptian. And these monarchs were neither exclusively queens nor named Candace. Candace is in fact no proper name at all but means queen, one of the few Ethiopian words identified. The sequence of rulers as determined by Reisner from the relations of their tombs does indeed show some queens including two rival queens who perhaps lived at the time of Petronius' invasion.[28] For the following century the data are still uncertain and the slight reference in Acts will have to wait for confirmation or identification of its Candace.

I may call attention to one other feature of the story, easily overlooked or unappreciated by the modern reader. Philip heard the Ethiopian reading, and yet he was reading to no audience but himself. He read to himself aloud. I am convinced that such was the universal practice in the ancient world. Even educated persons when quite alone read aloud, and practically never in silence. We are so used to silent reading that we hardly realize how literally we should take references like the one before us as typical of the ancient world. A few years ago Professor Hendrickson of Yale collected convincing evidence of this practice 'beginning', if I may use the words of Acts about Philip, 'from this very scripture.' Similar evidence was independently collected by Josef Balogh of Budapest in an article appropriately entitled *Voces Paginarum*.[29] It is pointed out that on the few occasions where silent reading is definitely mentioned in antiquity, it is mentioned as exceptional and as done for special reasons suggested in the context. Three of the instances are in Augustine. Another is the case where Augustus, wishing to rebuke certain *equites* mildly, arranged for them to receive a list of their wrongdoings in the presence of a committee of senators, which they were to read at once on the spot in silence. But for exceptions like these, reading even alone was oral and vocal. It is no wordplay when the ancients spoke of hearing the poets or Xenophon. In the story of the woman taken in adultery we read that Jesus wrote on the ground the sins of her accusers and when they *heard* they withdrew one by one (John 8 : 8, 9). Horace complaining of the loquacious boor who interrupts a man in solitude, describes the latter as either reading or silent. Evidently he was never both. Lucian describes the too rapid and superficial reader as one whose eye outstrips his voice. No wonder then that Philip *heard* the Ethiopian reading, and Philip need be no mindreader to know what it was he read.

The story of Paul's escape from Damascus in the next chapter of Acts brings us to another native monarchy outside the Roman Empire, the Arabian or Nabatean Kingdom. Acts with its usual anti-Jewish tinge says,

> 'The Jews made a plot to kill him, but their plot was known to Saul. And they were watching the gates day and night in order to kill him, but his disciples took him by night and let him down over the wall, lowering him in a basket' (9: 23-25)

But Paul himself gives the story,

> 'In Damascus the ethnarch of Aretas the king guarded the city of the Damascenes to seize me and I was let down in a basket through a window over the wall and escaped their hands' (2 Cor. 11: 32 f).

The stories are not completely contradictory, especially as the reference to the ethnarch of Aretas is obscure.

Aretas himself is a well known figure. There are numerous inscriptions of his and he is mentioned in literature. He is the fourth member of the dynasty that we know who bore the name, which he seems to have adopted in place of his good Greek Aeneas when he became king. Aretas is an Aramaic name, and is in the language which he used for his inscriptions. His non-hellenic character is shown further by his designation 'friend of his people', which doubtless was intended to contrast him with the usual royal titles of friendship for Rome or the Greeks. A predecessor called himself Aretas Philhellene. He was probably a half-conquered half-independent king but not so subservient to Rome as the Herods. He was in fact a rival of Herod Antipas though they were temporarily united by marriage. It was this Arabian princess, daughter of Aretas IV, whom Herod put away to marry Herodias. Since Aretas like Herod Antipas reigned until about A.D. 39, there is no chronological difficulty in fitting into the reign of Aretas the conversion of Paul and his escape from Damascus some three years later still.

But what of his authority at Damascus? An ethnarch is a somewhat unusual term in Greek and seems to have been used especially of national or tribal rulers in Syria and Arabia subject to a king or inferior in rank to a king. Minority groups in certain cities, like the Jews in Alexandria, had their ethnarchs, and the ethnarch of Aretas in Damascus would naturally be an Arab sheik or chieftain who headed the Arabian community in that mixed city. Without the version of the story in Acts we should never have thought of the ethnarch as being a Jewish ethnarch, and probably in spite of the frequency elsewhere of the term for a Jewish officer an Arabian is to be thought of.

There are three possibilities about an Arab ethnarch's part in the story. It is possible that the city of Damascus was actually at the time under Aretas' complete control. Both earlier and later it was certainly a Roman subject. Its coins under Tiberius and again under Nero have the imperial insignia but so far no coins for the reigns of Caligula and Claudius have been found, i.e. from A.D. 37 to 54. This is merely negative evidence. We do not know, though it is not impossible, that by gift or conquest Aretas recovered from the Romans the ancient city which certainly had been in Arab hands a century before.

A second possibility is that though controlled by Rome Damascus had a large semi-autonomous Arab population whose head was appointed by the Nabatean king. There was a large Jewish population in Damascus too. That too must have been organized for civil and religious life. And Acts itself tells us that Jews in Damascus were subject to arrest by warrants issued by the high priest in Jerusalem (9 : 2). Possibly from his distant capital at Petra Aretas exercised certain authority in Damascus through a local appointee.

The third possibility is that Aretas' ethnarch watched for Paul from the outside. In that case he was merely a chieftain not in the city but of the neighbourhood. It is obvious that whether the gates of a city are watched from the inside or the outside the best way to leave the city without detection is over the wall at another point in the city circuit. While therefore our knowledge of contemporary history does not yet clear up the relations of Aretas, the ethnarch, the city of Damascus and Paul, we recognize how close Acts brings us here to that Oriental strand in its environment, and if we choose we can solace ourselves by collecting evidence that Paul's simple but unceremonious means of escape from a walled city was not without parallel in ancient history. The escape of the spies at Jericho will come to mind, where we have in Josephus as in Acts the phrase over (literally, 'through') the wall without any mention of a window to which both the Septuagint there and Paul's letter here refers. Or one may mention the story told by Athenaeus of one Athenion, tyrant at Athens in the century before Paul, who 'set guards at the gates, so that many of the Athenians apprehending what was in store for them let themselves down over (literally, "through") the walls by night and fled'.[30]

The barbarian emerges again in the story at Lystra, where, after Paul had cured a man born lame,

'the crowd seeing what Paul had done raised their voice, saying in Lycaonian, "The gods have taken human form and come down to us." And they called Barnabas Zeus and Paul Hermes, because he was the leader of the speaking. And the priest of Zeus, which is before the city, brought bulls and garlands to the portals and wished to offer sacrifice with the crowd.' (14: 11-13)

Here we are in the heart of Anatolia. Paul has been preaching in the main to Jews as at Pisidian Antioch and Iconium, but threatened with hostility has escaped to the cities of Lycaonia, Lystra and Derbe. This whole territory was at the time part of the Roman province of Galatia—perhaps the very Galatians whom Paul reminds (Gal. 4: 14) that they had received him as a messenger of God. Unlike a northern part of the province, Galatia in the narrower sense, this part had no Celtic blood from the invading Gauls who had settled in Asia Minor two centuries before, but was part of the semi-Hellenized original stock of the tableland of Asia Minor. Augustus had constituted a row of cities, including Pisidian Antioch as well as Lystra, Roman colonies. That means that he had settled military veterans there and had hoped to guarantee peace against the neighbouring mountaineers. No doubt both Latin and Greek were spoken then at Lystra and Paul's speech which is reported later in Greek was doubtless given in that language. Why then does Luke mention that the old native language was used by the crowd? Probably he wishes to explain why Paul and Barnabas did not at once object to being called gods. They did not understand what was said; it was the action of preparing sacrifice which first made quite plain to them what the crowd was driving at— the bulls and garlands.

But in representing the Lycaonian language as breaking through, the historian's account is quite lifelike. These old dialects did survive though not much in written form. Little is known of Lycaonian except some place names like Lystra itself. It is referred to as late as the fourth century as still spoken there. The neighbouring districts like Cilicia and Phrygia had also their dialects and of the Phrygian language we know much more. Saint Jerome thought he could identify in Paul's Greek letters some Cilicisms.[31] The writer of Acts evidently intended here to indicate Lystra and Derbe as Lycaonian in contrast with Iconium from which they had fled as in some other area. This is doubtless correct though some contemporary writers spoke of Iconium as in Lycaonia. Xenophon, however, the first writer to mention Iconium, agrees with Acts in describing an eastward journey as coming 'to Iconium the last city of Phrygia' and 'thence through Lycaonia'.[32]

In view of the reference to the Lycaonian language it is particularly striking to find at once the names of Greek gods applied at Lystra to the missionaries and a reference to a temple of Zeus —or in even more characteristic form a temple of 'Zeus-before-the-City'. This seems written from a Greek point of view. There was a story in classical circles preserved by Ovid[33] of how in this very neighbourhood two peasants Baucis and Philemon were visited by Zeus and Hermes. Have the deities of Lycaonia been Hellenized by the author of Acts? Or did the Lycaonians, recognizing that their visitors were Greeks, call them by the names of Greek gods? And what were the names of the local deities if they were not already recognized by Greek names by the Lycaonians? A few years ago the view was expressed 'since they were talking Lycaonian it is very unlikely that they used the names Zeus and Hermes, or even that the temple in which they wished to sacrifice was really that of Zeus. Probably these Greek names represent native Lycaonian gods whose names are now lost'.[34] I am not so sure of that today. The Hellenization of the local gods of Asia Minor proceeded more rapidly than one might suppose. The continuation of publication of the inscriptions of Asia Minor suggests that even by the first century the Greek equivalents were accepted.

Thus though the names are now Greek it may be that they too as well as the reference to the Lycaonian speech are a reference to the barbarian element already overlaid. The easy suggestion of divinity which the mere wonder of the cure aroused is neither particularly Greek nor barbarian but characteristic of a credulous and pre-scientific age.

The last passage with which I shall deal as touching the Oriental world is the following scene of the shipwrecked Paul among the barbarians at Malta.

> And the foreigners showed us extraordinary kindness, for they lit a bonfire and brought us all to it because of the rainstorm which set in and because of the cold. And when Paul had twisted up a faggot of sticks and put it on the fire, a viper came out owing to the heat and fastened on his hand. And when the foreigners saw the snake hanging from his hand, they said to one another, 'Perhaps this man is a murderer, and though he has escaped from the sea, Justice did not permit him to live.' He, however, shook off the snake into the fire and suffered no harm. But they waited, expecting that he was going to swell up or fall down dead suddenly; but when they waited a long time and saw that nothing amiss was happening to him, they changed their minds and began to say that he was a god. Now in the neighbourhood of that place were properties belonging to the Chief of the island named Publius. And he took us in and entertained us hospitably for three days (28:2-7)

As in modern times, Malta was a pawn of empires, and the long stratification of cultures leaves some doubt as to what the natives were. The chief of the island was a Roman—the Publius whose father Paul cured of fever and dysentry. The name is too exact a Roman name to allow any other explanation. We can even confirm the simple but unusual title Chief or First ($\pi\rho\hat{\omega}\tau\sigma$) for the local officer of that island from a Latin inscription Mel(itensium) primus and from a Greek one $\pi\rho\hat{\omega}\tau\sigma\varsigma$ $M\epsilon\lambda\iota\tau\alpha\acute{\iota}\omega\nu$.

Though inscriptions in Malta are mainly Greek or Latin, first century bilingual inscriptions in Greek and Punic probably indicate the real language situation at that time. The island had been an ancient Phoenician colony, and even after Carthage was founded and had acquired the island for itself and had finally surrendered it to Rome, the Phoenician culture would remain. The underlying stratum of the story is Phoenician. This strand is of course Semitic like the Jewish and Arabian and has appeared, though we have not mentioned it, already elsewhere in Acts in connection with Cyprus. That too had a strong Phoenician background. No incident of Paul's visit on that island definitely refers to its Phoenician origin. Acts mentions only the Roman proconsul Sergius Paulus and a Jewish magician Bar-Jesus or Elymas and the two cities Paphos and Salamis, which whatever their origin, were sure to be mentioned by any Greek writer. More probably Phoenician in character are two names of Cypriotes who are mentioned elsewhere in Acts. Mnason is one of them, a Cypriote who was to entertain Paul on his overland journey from Caesarea to Jerusalem (21 : 16). He carries a Semitic sounding name, connected probably with the Jewish Menahem or Manaen and the Greek Mnaseas. The latter strikingly is borne by two other Cypriotes that we know of.

The other Cypriote named in Acts is Barnabas. The name Barnabas is increasingly appearing in Semitic inscriptions, most lately in the Dura Europos excavations on the Euphrates. Its two component parts are the familiar *bar* 'son of' and probably Nebo. Nebo is of course the old Assyrian deity which appears in Nebuchadnezzar, probably also in Abednego, as well as in many less familiar proper names. But Barnabion, Barnabas and like forms of the Christian period show how the name became established, Hellenized and internationalized.[35]

But to return to that other Phoenician island of the Mediterranean and Luke's account of the episode at Malta, I may repeat what I wrote some years ago:

It would be difficult to find a scene more full of the viewpoint of antiquity than this at Malta. The ancient Greek writer shows his own background in every line. Not only is the language idiomatic, but if one may say so, the ideas are idiomatic too. The natives, whatever their non-Hellenic tongue, are barbarians. Their alien speech foreboded to any Greek unfriendly treatment, especially to shipwrecked strangers. Their kindness is therefore merely one of the series of providential escapes of this charmed hero, not only from Jewish plots and the soldiers' plan to kill the prisoners as a last resort, but from the *inhospita Syrtis*, from shipwreck, from the savages, dreaded as pillagers of shipwrecks, and from serpent bite. The ideas he attributes to these barbarians are not, however, alien to the author himself. Any ancient would believe, were he 'Greek, Jew, barbarian, Scythian', that an escaped criminal could not evade his nemesis, though perhaps only a Greek or Roman would speak of Justice (Diké) personified. The fear of serpents and the typical test of religion that it can tread upon the adder and serpent, handle snakes and defy poison—this, too, is well known to every religion; and all these points could be illustrated profusely from ancient literature. To the examples collected in the commentaries others could be added.

The fickleness of the savages the author himself has illustrated in the reverse direction at Lystra. Unfortunately for Paul, on that occasion his deity was the first, not the last, guess of the changing Lycaonians. Luke also says that Jesus promised the Seventy 'the authority to tread upon serpents and scorpions'. As the treachery of American savages to every white man was assumed by our ancestors, so the inherent hostility of barbarians to Greeks was assumed quite as casually by Diodorus Siculus, when in describing the gold mines of Egypt he says that the prisoners were guarded by barbarians who could not be bribed through conversation or any friendly entreaty. In similar manner it was taken for granted by Andocides when he speaks of his own escape from shipwreck near 'a barbarian country where many who had come ashore had been killed after suffering the most cruel tortures'. To a contemporary like Dion of Prusa such unexpected hospitality would suggest by contrast the well-advertised barbarity of those ghouls who lived on dangerous leeward coasts battening on the loot of helpless human driftwood, or even like Nauplius luring mariners to their ruin. The murderer bitten in the hand would suggest to many readers the widespread idea of poetic justice that the member which sins is the part to receive punishment.

If the fear of barbarians is distinctively Hellenic, the same cannot be said of the superstitions about serpents. Here, for example, are just two passages from part of the literature of unadulterated Judaism, the Tosefta:

> They say concerning R. Chanina ben Dosa [c. 80 A.D.] that he was standing and praying and a serpent bit him and he made no pause. His disciples went and found it dead on the mouth of its hole (Berachoth iii. 20).
>
> R. Simeon ben Shatah [c. 80 B.C.] said, 'May I not see the consolation if I once did not see a man with a sword in his hand running after his fellow; the latter thereupon went into a deserted building followed by the other; I entered after him and found the one slain and a sword in the hand of the murderer dripping blood. . . . But he who knows the thoughts, he exacts vengeance from the guilty; for the murderer did not stir from the place before a serpent bit him so that he died' (Sanhedrin viii, 3).

Of course, the evangelist does not spoil his story by inquiring just what language these Maltese spoke. In spite of his evident interest in language, that would be a too modern curiositas. Nor does he stop to ask how the visitors knew their inner thoughts even if they spoke them aloud (in Punic?), nor whether then or later any poisonous serpents were to be found on that island. It was not even necessary for him to assure the reader that actual mirabilia occurred. Here and elsewhere in Luke-Acts the positive flavour of the antique and the supernatural is as conspicuous as is the absence of the modern rationalism.[36]

What I wrote then still serves my present purpose but I could now add more material. The objective and subjective factors in the story are by no means unique. Here for example is the quite modern incident from T. E. Lawrence's Revolt in the Desert:

> When the fire grew hot a long black snake wound slowly out into our group: we must have gathered it, torpid, with the twigs.[37]

The ineluctable character of justice, i.e. the goddess Diké, which I think is meant to underlie the remark about the escape from the sea I can further illustrate from a Greek schoolboy's writing exercise. As in more modern times, such copybook maxims are intended to point a moral. Here is what he wrote on such a maxim in the Fayoum on a piece of papyrus still preserved:

> A son having murdered his own father and fearing the laws fled into the desert. As he passed through the mountains he was pursued by a lion; and being pursued by a lion he went up into a tree, and finding a snake as he went up into the tree and being unable to go up on account of the snake he came down again. Wrong doing does not escape the attention of god.
> The divine always brings the wicked unto Diké.[38]

The last line is a verse of poetry. I think the rest was probably composed by the youth himself to illustrate it. The youth was writing in Greek in upper Egypt four or five centuries after Paul's shipwreck on Malta. But his thoughts are the thoughts of the ancients everywhere.

In summarizing this discussion of one aspect of the backgrounds of Acts it may be said: In the ancient as in the modern world cultures and ideas have no frontiers. There were in the setting of Luke's stories many features that can be classified as neither Greek, Roman, Jewish, nor Christian. Some of these may be described as universally human, some as specifically ancient, while others belong to quite definite strands inside or outside the Roman Empire—Ethiopian, Arabian, Phoenician, Anatolian. For some of them we may apply the collective name oriental, but in doing so we should recall that it but imperfectly sums up them all, that they go back to very ancient migrations to the West and to indigenous cultures. In that melting pot it was not true that

> *East is East and West is West*
> *And never the twain shall meet.*

In the time of Acts there was no oriental frontier either at the Euphrates or at the Bosporus. Even an imaginary frontier

c

would have to place most of the Eastern Mediterranean on the oriental side. Scratch beneath the skin of the other cultures and you will find the Oriental still there.

Behind temples or dedications to Roma and Augustus which, though not mentioned in Acts, greeted Paul at Mitylene and Samos and Athens and elsewhere is the traditional deification of kings; behind the Roman grain ships in which he sailed is the Egyptian maritime experience on the Nile and in the Red Sea; back of the Greek alphabet that he wrote is the Semitic alphabet; behind the Greek Zeus at Lystra is some Anatolian deity, acclaimed in Lycaonian speech; behind the Jewish magicians that he encountered in Ephesus and Cyprus lie Babylonian charms, just as behind the Greek *Genesis* which he quotes lie not only Hebrew but Assyrian folk tales. The holocaust of magical books following their owners' conversion is a form of behaviour which as book burnings in the present century remind us is not limited by time or cultural frontiers.[39] That it is located by our author precisely at Ephesus is no accident. The term 'Ephesian letters,' as magical words used in amulets had been called for centuries, gave that city a popular reputation for sorcerers and mountebanks that lasted down to Shakespeare's day.[40]

I am not going to add here a reference to the oriental mystery religions of which some New Testament scholars make so much. I see no reason to regard them as contemporary features of importance. The exotic phenomena that I have mentioned are more certain. They are at least enough for my present purpose.

What mixed names and backgrounds have the people that Paul meets! The Roman proconsul Gallio was born in Spain (Cordova), King Agrippa is of Idumean descent, while of Paul's associates Timothy is half Jew, half Greek, Silas has both the Semitic name and the Roman name Silvanus, Barnabas has the name of a Babylonian deity but is a Jewish Levite. Perhaps as a Cypriote some Phoenician blood flows through his veins. Aquila is a Jew of Pontus formerly resident in Rome and with a Roman name, while Apollos is an Alexandrian Christian with a reputation for Greek eloquence or learning who still taught the baptism of John. Such a world needed a universal religion and a missionary who could be 'all things to all men'.

NOTES TO CHAPTER I

1. On the relative unimportance of the author's identity for such studies as this see *The Making of Luke-Acts*, pp. 353-360, and below pp. 136f.

2. Cf. Richard Biscoe, *The History of the Acts of the Holy Apostles Confirmed from Other Authors*, London, 1742, 2 vols A. Wikenhauser, *Die Apostelgeschichte und ihr Geschichtswert*, 1921. W. M. Ramsay, *The Bearing of Recent Discovery on the Trustworthiness of the New Testament*, 1915, 1953.

3. *Beginnings of Christianity*, iv, pp. 245 f. The term νεωπιοιός is more widespread than was there suggested. See Pauly-Wissowa, *R.E.* xvi. 2433.

4. For example, Ronald Knox, Edgar J. Goodspeed, the late James Moffatt and Montague R. James.

5. *The Peril of Modernizing Jesus*, 1937.

6. They are also numerous. Harnack, *The Acts of the Apostles*, Eng. Trans., 1909, p. 125, notes that beside his three main classes of actors who are all mentioned by name and add up to about forty, 'there appear in the book about seventy other persons who are for the most part mentioned by name.'

7. For the parallels with Vettius Valens see F. F. Bruce, *The Acts of the Apostles*, 1951, *passim*, following E. K. Simpson, *Evangelical Quarterly*, ii, 1930, pp. 389 ff.

8. Luke and the Horse-Doctors, *Journal of Biblical Literature*, 52, 1933, 55-65.

9. P. Oxy iii, 475.

10. R. Herzog, Die Wunderheilungen von Epidauros, in *Philologus*, Suppl. XXII, Heft iii, 1931, pp. 14, 15, No. 11.

11. Since these lines were written Harvard University has been offered a collection of coins, selected to illustrate precisely the cities of Paul.

12. *Beginnings of Christianity*, v, 1933, p. 351.

13. Harnack, *Mission and Expansion of Christianity*, Book II, chapter vii Excursus.

14. Some discussions in English but not quite recent are Tenney Frank, Race Mixture in the Roman Empire, *American Historical Review*, 21, 1916, pp. 689-708; M. L. Gordon, The Nationality of Slaves under the Early Roman Empire, *Journal of Roman Studies*, 14, 1924, pp. 93-111; R. H. Barrow, *Slavery in the Roman Empire*, 1928, Chapter 8, The Mingling of Nations.

15. For a discussion on a wider scale see Martin P. Nilsson, The Race Problem of the Roman Empire, *Hereditas*, 2, 1921, pp. 370-389, reprinted in his *Opuscula Selecta*, Lund, vol. 2, 1952 (Svenska Institutet i Athen, *Skrifter*, 8° II. 2), pp. 940-964.

16. Mark 7: 26, but in Lucian, *Deorum Concilium* 4, Syrophoenician and Greek are opposites. Perhaps the gospel character was herself of mixed ancestry. For Greek as other than ethnic Greek cf. H. Windisch in Kittel, *Theologisches Wörterbuch zum neuen Testament* II. 506-508.

17. Juvenal iii, 62: *Iam pridem Syrus in Tiberim defluxit Orontes.*

18. Suetonius, *Cat.* 37, 5: *Roman sicut in sentinam confluxerant.* Cf. Tacitus, speaking of the Christians, *Ann.* xv, 44, 2. (Rome) *quo cuncta undique atrocia aut pudenda confluunt celebranturque.*

19. *Claud.* 25, 4. The passage is discussed below, pp. 94 and 115 f.

For a comprehensive account more judicious than the rhetoric of these ancient authors see G. La Piana, Foreign Groups in Rome, *Harvard Theological Review*, 20, 1927, 183-403.

20. *Beginnings of Christianity*, v, p. 61.

21. Cf. my *Making of Luke-Acts*, pp. 123-126.

22. A. Harnack, *The Acts of the Apostles* (Eng. Trans., 1909), p. 111.

23. An attractive suggestion has been made that the list is ultimately based on astrological geography, that is, on the doctrine that certain nations are under the several signs of the zodiac. There is such a list in Paulus Alexandrinus of the fourth century A.D. and evidence of one something like it earlier. They have striking resemblances with Acts in selection and order; for example, Armenia in Paulus and in the text of Acts of Tertullian and Augustine (in place of Judea). The author of Acts may not have been aware of such correspondence or such ultimate origin. He is more likely to have had twelve disciples in mind than twelve signs of the zodiac. But within the limited horizon of geography both the historian and the astrologer intend to suggest an enumeration that is inclusive with some circular sequence. See Stefan Weinstock, The Geographical Catalogue in Acts 2:9-11, in *Journal of Roman Studies*, 38, 1948, pp. 43-46, with the reference in his note 19 to a predecessor, J. Halévy.

24. There are also two word plays in the Greek of the brief passage quoted. One is between the place name Gaza and the same word for treasure (itself a Persian word). The other is between understand (γινώσκω) and read (ἀναγινώσκω) as in 2 Corinthians 3: 2, and frequently. Cf. below p. 48.

25. *N.H.*, vi, 186.

26. *Beginnings of Christianity*, iv, p. 96.

27. viii, 105.

28. G. A. Reisner, The Pyramids of Meroe and the Candaces of Ethiopia, in *Sudan Notes and Records*, v (1922), p. 175.

29. G. L. Hendrickson, Ancient Reading, in *The Classical Journal* (American), xxv, 1929, 182-196; J. Balogh, 'Voces paginarum,' *Philologus*, lxxxii, 1926, 84-109 and 202-240. I may add an illustration of my own, Lucian, *Imagines*, 10: 'You know, since you have often heard Xenophon praising.' It should not be overlooked that E. Norden who had stated this fact correctly but briefly in his *Antike Kunstprosa*, 1898, p. 6, gives in the Nachträge of the second and third reprints (1909, 1915) an interesting and growing set of examples including this passage in Acts.

30. Joshua 2: 1 ff., Josephus, *Antiq.* v, 1, 2 § 15, Athenaeus, *Deipnos.* v, 52, p. 214A. The story of Athenion was apparently taken by Athenaeus from Posidonius. It has other parallels to Luke's writings. See G. Rudberg, *Hellas och Nya Testamentet*, 1929, pp. 86-88 and in *Eranos*, 23, 1925, 200-203.

31. Hieron. *Epist.* 121, 10, 2-5, *ad Algasiam* (*P.L.* 22, col. 1029 f.).

32. *Anab.* i, 2, 19.

33. *Metam.* viii, 626 ff. The local fitness of the scene has been further in-

ferred from the inscriptions to these gods found in the neighbourhood. But as
for the first A. D. Nock (*Journal of Roman Studies*, 37, 1947, 106 note) argues
that the episode in Acts is 'hardly local folklore about divine visitants', as J. E.
Fontenrose had suggested in *Univ. Calif. Publications in Classical Philology*,
xiii, iv (1945), 105, but 'rather, a transformation of a story familiar in literature, to represent the Lycaonians as in effect saying "We are not going to
make the traditional mistake".' S. Eitrem has reminded us that the combination in cultus of Jupiter and Mercury may be attested in the mysteries of
Samothrace (*Coniectanea Neotestamentica*, iii, 1938, 12). It occurred also in
other places. If the story in Acts presents contemporary rather than local
colour it suits our present purpose quite as well.

34. *Beginnings of Christianity*, iv, p. 164.

35. See *Amicitiae Corolla*, ed. by H. G. Wood, 1933, p. 47 f. (Barnabas, etc.)
51 f. (Mnason, etc.).

36. *The Making of Luke-Acts*, pp. 341-344.

37. T. E. Lawrence, *Revolt in the Desert*, p. 107, cited as an illustration of
Acts 28 : 6-8 in *Expository Times* 46, 1935, p. 480.

38. E. Ziebarth, *Aus der antiken Schule*, 1910, No. 25, p. 14, from Grenfell
and Hunt, *Greek Papyri*, ii, 84.

39. For antiquity see A. S. Pease, Notes on Book-Burning in *Munera
Studiosa*, ed. by M. H. Shepherd, Jr., and S. E. Johnson, 1946, pp. 145-160.

40. *Comedy of Errors*, Act I, Scene ii, lines 97-102.

CHAPTER II

GREEK

The account of Paul's arrival at Malta, with which we closed the last chapter, contains one word which has been thought to reveal the Hellenic character of the author. Speaking in the first person plural he writes: 'And the foreigners showed us extraordinary kindness, for they lit a bonfire and brought us all to it' (28 : 2). The Greek word βάρβαροι, translated foreigners or barbarians, is of course the exact term by which the ancient Greeks distinguished all people outside their own circle. Here as often it implies especially a distinction of language—a matter in which our author elsewhere shows his sensitiveness; but applied as it is here either actually in contrast with himself or in sympathy with the Greek point of view it may be taken as a starting point for a study of his own Hellenic traits and the Hellenic elements in the story. In it we seem to see a little emergence of the national self-consciousness of the author. While the Greek-speaking Jews like Philo and Josephus do not hesitate to admit that as Jews they are barbarians, this writer puts Paul and his companions on the other side of the pale.[1]

Another suggestion of Greek sense of superiority occurs a little earlier, in a dialogue represented as taking place between Paul and the Roman military tribune after he was arrested in the temple court at Jerusalem:

Paul: May I say something to you?
Claudius Lysias: Do you speak Greek? What! Are you not the Egyptian who some time ago started a revolt and led into the desert four thousand men of the Sicarii?
Paul: I am a Jew, a Tarsian of Cilicia, a citizen of no mean city.

(21 : 37-39)

'A citizen of no mean city.' Not only is the phrase 'no mean' in form and application entirely idiomatic but it may be implied

from occurrences elsewhere that it is particularly expressive of
Greek pride. It would be like asking a man if he could speak
German and having him reply, 'Well, I was born in Hanover.'
Thus Dionysius of Halicarnassus writing in the first century
about pre-Roman Italian cities says: 'Cainina and Antemnae are
no mean cities, having Greek stock.' In other passages also 'not
mean' is shown in its context to imply pre-eminently Greek.[2]

Perhaps we are surprised to find the contrast made of Greeks
with Egyptians. The modern discovery of thousands of contemporary papyri in Egypt written in Greek by all classes of
society may have given us the impression that linguistically
Ptolemaic and Roman Egypt had become entirely Hellenized.
Of course we know from the abundant demotic papyri that the
native language was also used. The real difficulty here and elsewhere is that we are too inclined to judge the spoken language of
a country by its written remains. I have already referred to the
prevalence of Greek in the inscriptions of Lycaonia and Malta.
We are told however by Acts itself that the natives spoke in
another tongue. And so it may happen that in spite of written
Greek remains, the bulk of the population, especially in so far as
they were illiterate, in Judea, in Syria, in Rome, and in Egypt
spoke not the contemporary Greek but Aramaic, Syriac, Latin
and Egyptian demotic respectively.

Perhaps also Paul's reply represents more than a linguistic
correction. Does it not also voice a proud superiority over the
Egyptians felt by the well-born Tarsian apostle, or at least on his
behalf by an equally aristocratic biographer? That the native
Egyptian was thought little of by the Jews we know well from
Josephus. The Romans also scorned him, and Claudius Lysias
may well have shared and shown this feeling. Josephus again in a
somewhat exaggerated way speaks of the Egyptians as the only
people to whom the Romans, now lords of the universe, have
refused admission to any citizen rights whatever.[3] Of the Greek
attitude to Egyptians I may quote a phrase of protest by a Greek
writing to other Greeks, 'You are, my brothers, perhaps considering me a barbarian or an inhuman Egyptian.'[4]

Of course Luke's own language is his most obvious connection with things Greek. As has been just suggested it need not prove the thoroughness of his Hellenization, still less his native Greek origin. The degree of his Hellenic culture is of course difficult to determine. On the basis of his written style a strict purist would not grade Luke very high, but he is at least better than some other canonical writers and the changes he makes in paraphrasing Mark remind us of the advice of Moeris and Phrynichus in their handbooks of the right and wrong words to use, or of the corrections in a schoolboy's exercise which we occasionally find on the back of an old papyrus sheet or a broken piece of pottery.

An interesting fact about his style is its variation in itself. I can hardly escape the impression that it becomes more cultured, more truly Hellenic when his story, after the middle of Acts, launches out into the Greek speaking West. Why else does he spell Jerusalem otherwise than he has done before? Why else does he shift from Saul to Paul? And why do certain Greek constructions of more idiomatic character—genitive absolute for example, or litotes—of which the phrase 'no mean' or 'not insignificant' that has been mentioned is one—make their appearance first or most frequently in the second half of Acts?

The variations of style within Luke-Acts have been attributed to various causes, primarily the variant degree of semitism in the Greek of his sources. It has even been claimed that the author of Acts is not the author of Luke. A study of the data shows that the semitism is some of it deliberate and editorial, perhaps imitating the Septuagint, while the contrast in Greek is quite as marked between the first and second half of Acts as between Acts as a whole and Luke. It is in the second half of Acts that terms claimed to give that book a different and superior type of Greek really occur most frequently.[5] In other words, the sensitiveness to cultural differences which these chapters are here intended to stimulate, apparently operated naturally in the original author himself in such a way as to leave its imprint in the very flavour of his language in his ongoing narrative.

To be sure Professor Torrey of Yale had another explanation.[6] He believed that beginning after the preface to his Gospel and continuing up to the middle of Acts Luke is translating continuously from the Hebrew or Aramaic of his written sources, and translating so literally, so closely and even so inaccurately that we can still detect the semitic cast of the underlying original. At last by Acts 16 he becomes himself and writes in his own untrammelled style.

But even if Torrey is right, we have at least in the end of Acts good evidence for the cultural level of Luke's Greek. If these chapters, or at least the so-called 'we' passages, are due to a written source as used to be supposed, it is not likely that that source is responsible for the style of Luke here, and that the final editor himself belonged to a lower level of style. Whatever his sources were, he himself is no Aramaic speaking Semite like the dwellers in Jerusalem. In the very beginning of Acts he makes that clear. He says that the scene of Judas' death, Akeldama in Aramaic, was so called 'in their language'—evidently not his own (1 : 19).

It is worth while to emphasize, what perhaps ought to have been always taken for granted, that the language of Luke-Acts fits well within our knowledge of contemporary Greek. The more one reads of the latter the more evident this likeness becomes. For a student of Acts this is a delightful experience, this increasing feel of the naturalness of its language and the idiomaticalness of certain of its expressions as one keeps meeting them in other literature or even in unliterary sources. I wish it were possible to illustrate this extensively but both lack of space and the difficulty of presenting such material prevent my doing so. Canon W. L. Knox[7] has made some discriminating comments on the Greek of Acts, to which those qualified to savour the more or less Greek quality of Luke's vocabulary and grammar may be referred.

One of the errors and dangers of the over eager study which the New Testament has received has been the excess of interest in the occurrence or non-occurrence of New Testament words in other writings. It is impossible at this distance to be sure as to what words are really significant in Luke's vocabulary. Both where it coincides with another's vocabulary and where it does not coincide, we are usually in the presence of nothing more than accidents. It is perhaps mere chance, added to a general similarity of date and style, which leads to certain likenesses between Luke and the writer of Second Maccabees in our Old Testament apocrypha.[8] They are both in our Greek Bible and so the likeness is most impressive to students who concentrate on that volume. But there are of course affinities farther afield.

There was the same fault with that most ingenious of arguments which attempted to confirm the tradition that these books were written by a physician named Luke by the evidence of words which he uses which were also in the great Greek medical Corpus. Now it is natural that Galen the voluminous Greek writer on disease should employ many words that were also used a century before by our author, and perhaps not used in the limited vocabulary of the other writers of the New Testament. Time is confirming the verdict of such a trustworthy scholar of the history of the Greek language as Albert Thumb:

'The fact that St. Luke makes use of medical terms found in Hippocrates and other physicians in no way implies a study of medical writings ("Luke the physician"), but only some acquaintance with the ordinary terminology of his age; many such medical words, indeed . . . had passed into such general use in the vernacular that they prove nothing more than St. Luke's familiarity with the language of his time.'[9]

It is equally erroneous to look at the unique words in Acts as significant, the so-called ἄπαξ λεγόμενα. Discoveries are regularly reducing their number; what remain unparalleled are also what Deissmann calls a 'statistical accident'. May I mention some discoveries of recent times—or at least cases that have come to my attention since the commentary on Acts was published early in 1933.

In the speech at Athens, God is spoken of as fixing the boundaries of men's residence. In the familiar version it runs 'he hath determined the times appointed and the bounds of their habitations' (17: 26). The Greek noun ὁροθεσία, 'bounds,' which means not merely boundaries but rather the actual setting up of boundaries or the determination of frontiers, was formerly said not to be found elsewhere. In 1906 was published an inscription from Priene containing the word. This was noted by Moulton and Milligan in their *Vocabulary*, *s.v.* But they overlooked apparently an instance in a Berlin papyrus of A.D. 151 though it was published in 1903.[10] These three instances of the compound make it almost certain that a form in Galen[11] should be so accented as to come from the same word, though the scholars who were on the lookout for medical examples evidently missed this one. I had called attention to all this before,[12] but more recently I came upon another example, the closest in date to Acts of any. On a large slab found *in situ* in modern Rumania was recorded in Greek and Latin a series of decisions by Roman *legati* on the boundaries of the old Milesian colony of Histria at the mouth of the Danube on the Black Sea. The decisions of former officials are here confirmed by Marius Laberius Maximus on 20 October, A.D. 100. This inscription was found in 1915 and published shortly after in the *Annales* of the Rumanian Academy at Bucharest. It begins with a headline in bold Greek letters:

The fixing of boundaries (ὁροθεσία) of Laberius Maximus.[13]

In the account of Peter's vision at Joppa prior to his visit to the centurion Cornelius we read that he 'became hungry' (10: 10). That natural English word for a natural human feeling translated a Greek compound which, though regularly formed, has long graced the list of 'words peculiar to the New Testament'. In the Commentary I wrote: 'πρόσπεινος is one of the small and diminishing number of words in Acts which have not yet been found elsewhere.' But the latest edition of Liddell and Scott's *Greek-English Lexicon* (p. 1523) quietly records an instance coming from a writer of the same century as Acts and—though his profession deserves I think no emphasis—from one of the most famous eye doctors of antiquity, one Demosthenes who studied medicine at Laodicea.

The account of Herod's death has much in it that is characteristic of the Hellenistic world. To be eaten with worms was not a normal form of disease but reserved as a peculiar divine retribution for those who, like this vainglorious prince, offended the gods with their pride and blasphemy. But the word employed by Acts 12: 23, σκωληκόβρωτος, literally worm-eaten, occurs nowhere in literature except in Theophrastus, a writer on plants who applies it to diseased grain. Some have asserted that it was a technical term of medicine or else that this author himself invented it. The critics cannot have it both ways at once,—technical and unique. The publication of an instance in the papyri, and of another instance of its opposite 'unworm-eaten', —in both cases applied to grain—seemed to confirm its popular agricultural rather than its technical and medical usage. So I wrote in 1926. But in the four years that followed, four volumes of papyri were published contributing each one further instance of the word, again in agricultural connections—in one instance the still longer compound 'whole-worm-eaten'.[14]

In an account of Paul's address on the Temple stairs Acts describes his interruption by the auditors as follows: 'they were howling and waving their garments and throwing dust into the air' (22: 23). The phrase 'waving their garments', literally throwing their cloaks, is not perfectly clear. In a long additional note on dust and garments I discussed the several gestures in Acts connected with these objects and for the passage under consideration guessed at the meaning above, though as Field had observed before, 'there is no good example of this use' of the verb ῥιπτεῖν. The example I have now to add is scarcely perfect since the papyrus from which it comes is broken. It belongs as one of the more recent accessions to some documents of which I shall speak again—the so-called 'heathen martyr acts' of Isidore. In the colourful scene before the emperor Claudius, when the dignified Alexandrian gymnasiarch dressed in his official regalia is being led away to execution, the rhetor makes some gesture with his hand and 'tossed his cloak' (verb and noun the same as in Acts).[15]

There is no reason to suppose that Luke was acquainted much with Greek literature because he knew the Greek language. Unlike some of his literary contemporaries he does not quote the Greek poets freely. Still less like Josephus's literary assistant and the Atticists does he imitate their style. Nor do such echoes as we find indicate that the New Testament writer knew at first hand the literature cited. Beside Aratus and Epimenides of whom I must speak later in connection with the scene at Athens it has been supposed that in Acts are echoes of Euripides and Homer, while the genuine letters of Paul have at the most a single identified Greek quotation—the line in 1 Corinthians (15: 32) from Menander: 'Evil communications corrupt good manners,' or better translated, 'Bad company ruins good morals.' If we accept all these at face value they do not probably carry us further than the category of familiar quotations or at most familiar authors. Concerning the latter we have now some contemporary information. The literary papyri give us from Egypt a kind of straw vote as to the popularity of Greek authors if we count the number of pieces surviving for each of them. The returns reported in one tabulation[16] ran as follows:

Homer	-	-	282
Demosthenes	-	48
Euripides	-	-	32
Menander	-	-	26
Plato	-	-	-	23

A later and fuller listing of papyrus fragments and extending down through the Sixth Century[17] shows these leaders in very much the same ratio to each other, with Hesiod and Isocrates perhaps deserving to be included in the list as occurring as frequently as Plato and Menander. Now three of these five leaders have already been mentioned. Were it necessary for me to suggest possible echoes in Luke-Acts of the other two—Demosthenes and Plato—I think I could do so.[17a]

What other aspects of ancient life beside language and literature can be called Hellenic it is difficult to say. The strands of culture have so interwoven themselves that Greek ideas and Greek institutions no longer stand apart in the complex of ancient civilization.

While not necessarily Greek, Luke's emphasis on cities may point in that direction. While Paul in his letters uses the names of

Roman provinces, Acts tells the story of Paul as largely carried on from city centres. Even in the earlier parts of his narrative where Judea is the setting, he talks more of cities than do the other evangelists. The full evidence cannot be displayed here and now.[18] I would call attention to the fact that for the census of Quirinius he represents everyone as returning to his own city, the crowd at the feeding of five thousand as coming from every city, with regard to the law of Moses he speaks of it as being read in every city, and that for Paul bonds and afflictions are predicted in every city. He indicates that persons in his story or previous events belong in the city. He is not satisfied to name merely the district from which a person comes, but often the city, for example Paul a Tarsian (9: 11), or a Tarsian of Cilicia (21: 39; 22: 3). Lydia is not merely a Lydian as we should expect but also of the city of Thyatira (16: 14), Sopater is a Berean (20: 4), Aristarchus is called a Macedonian (19: 29) but in another passage a Thessalonian (20:4). So Trophimus is called an Asian, but in another passage an Ephesian (21: 29). Gaius the Macedonian (19: 29) is according to a modern textual preference[19] described as Gaius from Doberus (a rather obscure location in Macedonia). Very idiomatic too is the phrase 'the parts of Libya about Cyrene' (2: 10). It is Cyrene the city that gives the name to the district.[20]

For Greeks the geographical unit is the city. Politically also the older city institutions were allowed in the Roman Empire to keep their place. Of course in Roman colonies this was not the case, and Luke mentions several of these, in Philippi calling it (rather unusually) by its Latin term *colonia* and mentioning (in Greek terms) its main magistrates the *praetores* or *douviri* and their attendants the *lictores*. But although elsewhere the city institutions were Greek they were by no means as uniform in the Greek cities as in the Latin colonies. Just as you can test a man's knowledge of modern Oxford and Cambridge by his ability to name correctly the presiding officer of each college whether as Master, Principal, Provost, Warden, Rector, President or Dean, or one's knowledge of old Germany's political constitution when over three hundred territorial sovereignties existed within the

Holy Roman Empire ruled by kings, electors, and princes, counts and counts palatine, dukes and grand dukes, landgraves, margraves and all the rest, so one can test Luke's knowledge of municipal institutions in the Aegean cities. His language fully meets the test.

At Thessalonica for example he calls the officers *politarchs*, a word used nowhere else in ancient literature. But the correctness of his terminology is completely vindicated by the Macedonian inscriptions in the centuries before and after the Christian era. Some fourteen instances of the noun or verb are found in them (five cases from Thessalonica alone). Indeed except in Macedonia and the neighbouring countries we have scarcely any evidence of the use of the word at all. It was a local term or title. As in Acts, the epigraphical evidence shows that the office was not held by one person each year but they formed a multiple magistracy— in Thessalonica five or six at a time. It is said that spanning a street in modern Salonika there stood until recent times a first century marble arch with an inscription that begins with the participle πολιταρχούντων followed by the names of six magistrates.[21]

At Ephesus on the other hand Acts refers to the principal municipal officer as town-clerk (γραμματεύς). The excavations at Ephesus by the British and Austrian expeditions, though still partly unpublished and also incomplete, give us a flood of light on the local colour of this scene—the theatre in which the town meetings were held, both impromptu and regularly, the worship of Artemis and the trades it encouraged of what we should call 'accessories', and among other things precisely the use of the same term town-clerk for the democratic city's executive officer. The coins and inscriptions of Ephesus show the high municipal place he occupied. Indeed generally in Asia Minor he was the officer whose administration dated the year—the eponymous magistrate.

But the same passage mentions other officers and gatherings than the town clerk and town meeting. There were in Ephesus also, we are told, sessions and proconsuls. The latter is of course the name for the governor of a senatorial province, though if the writer of Acts intends us to believe that more than one proconsul held office at a time in the province of Asia he is quite mistaken. The office was a single appointment of indefinite tenure, usually not more than two years. Elsewhere the same author gives the name to a single incumbent, quite correctly using the singular and connecting him with the provincial capital, as to Sergius Paulus at Paphos, proconsul of Cyprus, and to Gallio at Corinth, proconsul of Achaia. Unlike some other provinces mentioned in Acts which were neither continuously nor intermittently treated as 'imperial' and governed by *legati*, Cyprus and Asia were from the time of Augustus on always senatorial, that is governed by proconsuls while Achaia had become a senatorial province for the second time in A.D. 44. Indeed the two proconsuls named are mentioned elsewhere in inscriptions.[22] It is unfortunate that in Ephesus the author's reference to them is so vague.

There is another plural in the story of Ephesus—again unfortunately without personal names. We read that when the riot was taking place Paul wished to go to the people 'and some of the Asiarchs who were friends of his sent to him and begged him not to venture into the theatre.'

The plural here causes no difficulty, and the name correctly used introduces us to a political institution that existed alongside of the Roman provincial government and the Greek municipal government, that is the κοινόν, or commune, or council of the cities of Asia. Such councils are well known in both the east and the west of the Empire. They included the principal cities of a province, which by delegates chose annually the head of the council—called Asiarch, Galatarch, Lyciarch, etc.—and other officers. Ephesus as one of the most important cities in the Asian κοινόν would have, including former incumbents, several Asiarchs.[23] The word, though, like politarchs, it is rare in literature, is frequently met with in inscriptions. The duties of the council were from the first religious as well as political, and under the Empire it maintained the cult of the reigning Emperor and Roma in various cities. The reference in Acts is therefore of interest as coming the nearest in that book and perhaps the nearest anywhere in the New Testament to mentioning the emperor worship of the age. It is tantalizing, now that our knowledge and interest in the cult of the emperors is so increased, that the New Testament writers make no explicit reference to it. Luke's reason for mentioning the Asiarchs at all is not their religious association. Of course it would be of interest to know that to officers of the imperial cult Christianity did not seem an enemy, even though in the reverse direction tolerance or approval would be less likely. Rather, if we may conjecture from his behaviour elsewhere, our author would be concerned to show that political authorities were friendly disposed to Paul and his work. As to Gallio in Achaia or to the procurators Pilate, Felix and Festus in Judea no political or criminal charges against the heralds of the gospel seemed serious or relevant, so Paul seemed innocent to the jealous supporters of Roman authority in the province of Asia. The Asiarchs were Paul's friends—whatever the proletariat of Ephesus felt about him.

Furthermore our author is not above a sense of pride in the social standing of Paul's converts. Now the Asiarchs were undoubtedly some of the 'best people' in Ephesus—the richest and the most élite. As with many Greek municipal appointments, only the possession of considerable means made one eligible to be an Asiarch. It is perhaps a mark of Luke's Greek viewpoint that this timarchic or economically aristocratic emphasis occurs so often in reference to the Apostles' converts. It was a royal treasurer in Ethiopia, a member of Herod's σύντροφοι at Antioch, leading women or wives of leading men at Thessalonica, women of position and the chief men of Antioch, an Areopagite at Athens, women of position in Berea and the like, who accepted the gospel elsewhere.[24] The speech of Paul in Jerusalem was delivered to a notable gathering: 'Agrippa and Bernice came with great pomp and went into the audience-chamber with the tribunes and the chief men of the city'—the city's gentlemen of pre-eminence. The phrase seems to bespeak both the metropolitan and the aristocratic viewpoint. It was therefore worth noting that the Asiarchs of Ephesus were friends of Paul and were concerned for his safety.

For Greek colouring in Luke's writings we naturally look to

D

his story of Paul in Greece proper and we do not look in vain. Corinth to be sure was no longer a typically Greek city and such references to Paul's experience there in Acts or in his epistles suggest Roman rather than Greek history. The proconsul Gallio has been mentioned. His 'judgment seat' has been identified in the ruins of the ancient city by modern archaeologists. It was a magnificent affair. But it was built in Roman times and with Roman models.[25] Even the city was a Roman colony. Paul apparently (Rom. 16: 23) mentions a municipal officer οἰκονόμος τῆς πόλεως named Erastus. It is barely possible that he is the same as the Erastus mentioned in Acts 19: 23 and the Erastus of 2 Tim. 4: 20 and also the Erastus of an inscription found near the theatre at Corinth. But the inscription is in Latin and refers rather to a Roman title of *aedile*.[26] Almost the only Latin word used by Paul in his Greek letters is the *macellum*, or meat market at Corinth.[27] This word also is now found in some Latin inscriptions dug up there. The excavators have uncovered now the Roman market itself. Yes, when Corinth, the eye of Greece, was extinguished by Mummius in 146 B.C. its Greek history was over. A century later Julius Caesar founded rather a Roman city, *Colonia Laus Iulia Corinthiensis*.[28]

But for Athens the history was different. Its art treasures had not, like those of Corinth, been all carried off to Rome. It was never destroyed, though it suffered severely during and after the siege of Sulla in 88-86 B.C., as recent excavation has made plain. Its historic memories lingered. There is every reason to think that the author of Acts knew and felt something of this Greek tradition. His account is familiar. Paul arrived alone at Athens. He viewed its idols and other objects of devotion, including an altar with the inscription to an Unknown God. He met not only the Jews in the synagogue but Greeks in the Agora or market place. Stoic and Epicurean philosophers were among his auditors. The general attitude was a mixture of curiosity and mockery. They thought him a preacher of new deities—and particularly scoffed at the resurrection from the dead. Finally he was brought before the Areopagus, but received no definite condemnation or acquittal. One of the members of that body, Dionysius the Areopagite, is named as among his converts, also a woman (the Western text may have called her a woman of position) named Damaris. The author of Acts gives in abstract the contents of such a speech as Paul might have made there,— a much admired and recently much discussed, composition.[29]

Now in all this it is difficult to believe that the author is not aware of the local and intensely Greek setting which he has at hand. I will not say that the style is more classical than in other parts of the book, though a few choice λέξεις 'Αττικαί have been detected as well as some quite rare words. But rare words are not necessarily classical, and indeed perhaps the feeling of the passage is more typically expressed by the epithet that his supercilious hearers apply to Paul, which though neither rare nor classical is characteristic of the dilettante. A babbler or a gossip or a cock sparrow are English attempts to render the word σπερμολόγος.

The appropriateness of the reference to philosophers at Athens is also evident. That was the traditional home of philosophy, and the Stoics and Epicureans were the leading schools of the time. Josephus in writing about Judaism to Greeks of the same period deals with the Pharisees and Sadducees largely in terms of the philosophic beliefs which these two leading philosophical sects quarrelled about. In fact our author may be intending to represent Paul as appealing to one side rather than the other here just as in a later scene he appears as trying to secure the support of the Pharisees against the Sadducees in his belief in the resurrection of the dead (23 : 6-10). For a parallel to Luke's story one may mention the highly satirical skit of Lucian's entitled 'Zeus in High Tragedy'. At Athens in the Painted Porch there was a debate going on attended by a large reputable body of spectators, to which Zeus himself became a witness incognito, disguised as a philosopher. Damis the Epicurean and Timocles the Stoic were debating, the former denying the existence of gods or of any divine care for man, the latter supporting the doctrine of Providence. Among the Stoic's arguments were various lines of approach but they included 'the order of the created world, the sun always travelling the same road and the moon in like manner and the changing seasons and plants growing and animals being born and these all so very skilfully devised.' He also argued 'if there are altars there are also gods. But there are altars, so then there are also gods.' His opponent ridiculed all his arguments, mentioning the tomb of Zeus at Crete among other evidences against the existence of the gods. Finally, as in the story of Paul, the crowd dispersed eager to hear the debate continued on the following day.[30]

Better evidence of a sense of fitness of the passage to circumstances is the author's use in the speech of quotation from the poets. As this writer makes his speakers in Jewish synagogues or Palestinian scenes have recourse to the Old Testament scriptures for texts, so here Paul is pictured as quoting Greek poets, as the original says emphatically 'some of your own group'.[31] As Origen quaintly says he becomes to those without the law as without the law, turning to his own purpose the saying of the poet, 'From Zeus do we begin; his race are we'.[32] Of course the use of such quotations is no evidence that either Paul or the writer of Acts had wide or first hand knowledge of Greek literature. Probably many college undergraduates today have read more of it. And it is perhaps significant that the words 'For we also are his offspring' were already current in a poem of Cleanthes when Aratus included them in the fifth line of his *Phaenomena*. The latter became well known in the later centuries when Luke wrote and of course the first lines are always better known than the rest.

The poetical influence may extend further in this speech than the single quotation. Syriac writers, apparently dependent on Theodore of Mopsuestia,[33] assert that other words of the speech are a quotation: 'In him we live and move and have our being.' Indeed they combine them with some words about the Cretans in another New Testament work, the Epistle to Titus, so that we get a whole quatrain:

> *They carve a tomb for thee, O holy and high one,*
> *The Cretans always liars, evil beasts, slow bellies;*

For thou art not dead for ever but alive and risen,
For in thee we live and move and have our being.

The second line which is the one quoted in Titus (1 : 12) is attributed by Clement of Alexandria to Epimenides the Cretan. If the whole belongs together he is also then the author of the fourth line quoted in Acts and the quatrain is a criticism of the Cretan tomb of Zeus.[34]

Some doubt has been thrown upon this whole theory but there are two or three interesting coincidences beside the coincidence of having attributed to Paul by different writers the second and fourth lines of one stanza. One is that the actual Greek text of part of the remaining two lines is extant in Chrysostom quoted indeed from Callimachus but substantially the same in thought and wording,

For the Cretans have fashioned thy grave, O Lord,
But thou dost not die but livest forever.

The second is that the inscription 'To the Unknown God' has its closest contact with history in the story of the same Epimenides the Cretan visiting Athens and ridding it of the plague by propitiating the unknown gods by sacrifices on anonymous altars. The third is that the words in Acts if actually quoted from a poem to Zeus contain that very common Greek word play between the name Zeus and the verb ζάω 'live'. Of course the English reader and indeed most modern Greek readers miss the word play—but the ancient reader, to whom all word plays were most natural and this one particularly familiar, would readily see that a quotation is intended 'In him we live and move and have our being' and that the etymological argument is: He is called Zeus 'living'. A tomb for him is a lie. He is alive himself and we live in him.

It is strange that this word play has not attracted the notice of commentators. One might think they would have guessed long ago that the phrase 'in him we live and move and have our being' was quoted from a poem about Zeus. When we read for example in the Latin play of Plautus 'Juppiter ... per quem vivimus' we may be almost sure that the Greek originally had Zeus and ζῶμεν, i.e. Zeus through whom we live. The evidences for this word play on Zeus and 'live' in Greek and even Syriac had been sporadically mentioned before. Only in 1933 was anything like an adequate list compiled and published by Otto Weinreich[35] of some thirty instances in ancient literature, but not including this passage in Acts or Epimenides. Yet there can be no doubt that in this single innocent 'live' here, half of an incomplete word play survives, and the original pagan and polytheistic elements of the quotation shine through the Christian monotheism of Acts as the Greek word play shines through the Latin of Plautus. Nor do I think we need doubt that the Christian writer recalls it. It would not be uncongenial to his mentality (note Gaza the city in Acts 8 : 26, and γάζα treasure in the next verse, and in the same context the common Greek and Latin word play between 'read' and 'know') and was as I have said a Greek commonplace. The Jew with his prejudice against paganism might find more congenial the opposite word play between Apollo and 'destroy'[36] but the Jew himself both in early times and in later time, as Genesis and Philo teach us, had his own interest in the etymology of proper names, and at the very beginning of his scriptures indulges in the analogous word play. 'And the man called his wife's name Eve; because she was the mother of all living.' A Hellenistic Jew impersonating the Greek Aristeas uses both this word play and the equally frequent one between Δία accusative of Zeus and διά the preposition 'on account of'. The Jews, he writes, 'worship God the overseer and creator of all things, as all men do, though we (Greeks) name him Δία and Ζῆνα. For so the original men not inappropriately indicated that he on whose account all things are made to live and come to being is both ruler and lord over all.'[37]

Before leaving the 'poets' a word of caution is necessary. There can be no doubt that the phrase 'His race are we' is a definite quotation. The full text of Aratus' *Phaenomena* is extant and the author of Acts professes to be quoting. It is by no means so certain that the phrase 'In him we live and move and are' is a quotation, though as we have seen modern scholars assign it to a definite author (Epimenides) and context (the tomb of Zeus).

They have even tried to identify the name of the poem (Cretica) and the speaker of the lines (Minos).[38]

There are some doubtful links in this chain. The indefinite plural 'some' used in citing the poets is characteristic of the ancient method of quoting a single and known passage.[39] Some often means one. The quoter himself is not in doubt about his source. Hence we need not seek here in Acts any plurality of poets of a single saying (Aratus *and* Cleanthes) or any plurality of quotations (one before and one after the citation). When two passages are quoted they usually follow each other after the citation and are connected by 'and'.

The words are only indirectly attributable to Epimenides. They sound Stoic rather than more ancient. At least that is the opinion of M. Pohlenz and A. D. Nock, who have judgment in such matters. We have seen how they are associated also with words attributed to Callimachus. There were no quotation marks in antiquity nor any copyright. The poets freely borrowed from each other. This is shown by the associated bits of verse. If Titus 1 : 12 is derived from the *Theogony* or *Oracles* of Epimenides, that is an echo of Hesiod's *Theogony* and is in turn echoed in the Hymn to Zeus by Callimachus. Another hymn to Zeus by Cleanthes is perhaps the source of the phrase from Aratus. That may have both earlier (Homer) and later (Posidonius) literary pedigree. That early Christian commentators regarded the words 'In him we live and move and are' as quoted and tried to connect them with another New Testament passage should not be decisive for us. It is possible that instead of being a quotation they are really due to Luke (or Paul). The author of Acts would be quite capable of writing them without any exact pagan or Christian source. As he can both quote the Septuagint and compose in·Septuagint style, as we see in the Canticles of Luke 1 and 2, and in speeches in Acts, so he can probably both quote Greek poetry like Aratus and compose in Greek poetic style. Would it be claiming too much to say that even in reporting the words of Jesus in the Gospel he has made slight alterations and additions with matching material rather than with alien patching? Throughout the scene at Athens the language has the right

Greek colouring. The same is true of the other and briefer address of Paul to Gentiles, the speech at Lystra. Speaking again of God's relation to men he says, 'Yet he did not leave himself without witness, for he did good and gave you from heaven rains and fruitful seasons' (14 : 17). I have often wondered whether a lost Greek poem is echoed here. There are certainly poetical expressions.[40] If instead of quoting, the author himself both here and in the scene at Athens is doing some 'invisible weaving' in Greek poetic style, our evidence of his relation to Greek culture is no less convincing than if he is actually quoting. In either case the passages fit our present subject, the Hellenic element in Acts.

It is unnecessary to suppose that if the altar to the Unknown God goes back to the story of Epimenides, the author of Acts knew that connection. We have evidence that such an altar at Athens was known about by others who do not know or do not mention the origin of it. The story as it has come down to us probably means that the Athenians failing to reach the effective deity under any of the known names, adopted the natural expedient of offering sacrifice to the deity responsible for the plague anonymously.[41] Such superstitious inclusiveness is a mark to other writers of the religiousness of Athens. Philostratus for example comments on the folly of Hippolytus for insulting the goddess Aphrodite. It would be more prudent, he says, to speak well of all the gods, and especially in Athens where are established altars even of unknown gods. The religiousness of the Athenians was proverbial, and our own author refers to the abundance of idols there, and represents Paul as citing the inscription as a mark of what the King James version translated as their 'too superstitious'—we should say 'ultra religious'—character.

In spite of this general verisimilitude of the account—at least its accordance with other contemporary impressions of Athens—some scholars have questioned whether the whole story is not borrowed from a purely secular source rather than based on Christian history[42] and in particular whether the inscription on the altar is not deliberately misread. Jerome says, 'The inscription on the altar was not, as Paul asserted, to the unknown god but as follows: To the gods of Asia and Europe and Africa, gods unknown and foreign. But since Paul did not need several gods but only one unknown god he used the singular word.'

Jerome compares such adaptation of the inscription to Paul's use of the verses of heathen poets. It is almost surely true that the poetical quotations in Acts that we have discussed have been changed to fit the context from 'thy' to 'his' and possibly from 'thee' to 'him'. But a change of number in a brief inscription from 'gods' to 'god' is rather more bold than a change from second to third person. We can probably never say positively that no altar in Athens bore the exact phrase in the singular, though nearly all the evidence we have suggests the plural. If the singular is unhistorical it may be due to editorial treatment or even to the inaccuracy of memory. More extraordinary inaccuracies have occurred in perfectly good faith. I am thinking, for example, of the famous statue of Christ in the Andes set up to mark a covenant of peace between Chile and Argentina. From 1905, a year after it was dedicated, until 1932 writers both in Spanish and in English declared with no one to gainsay them that there is inscribed at its base the words 'Sooner shall these mountains crumble to dust than the people of Argentina and Chile break the peace to which they have pledged themselves at the feet of Christ the Redeemer'. But the inscription simply is not there. Neither can photographs reveal it nor recent tourists confirm it. It is merely a quotation made from the peroration of a speech delivered at the dedication by Archbishop Ramon Angel Jara.

Still more dubious is the sentimental association of Paul's speech with the present barren hilltop called the Areopagus or Mars Hill at Athens. I am not questioning the accuracy of the present name nor am I denying that Acts quite appropriately speaks of Paul as standing in the midst of the Areopagus and delivering his famous address. But the modern traveller who sits there, Testament in hand, and looks wistfully across to the neighbouring Parthenon on the Acropolis, 'the glory that was Greece,' must be informed that the Areopagus spoken of was no longer the actual hill of Mars but the court which formerly met there and which still bore the name of its earliest place of assembly. The persistence of such a court into Roman times is sufficiently attested even though its history and later functions are obscure. It was well known abroad and perhaps mention of it may therefore be more due to historical reminiscence and current reputation than to the author's actual contact with events. One can only tentatively compare it with the town clerk in Ephesus and the politarchs in Thessalonica as evidence of acquaintance with contemporary local administration. Just why it should deal with Paul is uncertain. Ramsay thought it was a censor of public instruction, others that Paul was asked to prove the political inoffensiveness of Christianity. Both views may be mistaken. Nor can we even yet provide the sentimental sightseer with a new locale in the monuments of ancient Athens for the scene. The Royal Portico (στοά βασίλειος) where the council probably met was the first of a series of buildings which Pausanias, who visited Athens shortly after Paul, described in order as you approach the city from the Ceramicus. Some years ago when I was at Athens it was thought that the excavations of the American School of Classical Studies had just uncovered its site. Further discoveries have made it probable that the court met in a slightly different part of these buildings and sometimes outside the Agora entirely.[43]

There remains one more aspect of Luke's scene in Athens that seems to me to suggest local colour. That is the charge against Paul, described here but nowhere else in Acts as of bringing in new gods. No reader of Plato's *Apology* or of Xenophon's *Memorabilia* is likely to miss the resemblance to the charge against Socrates—that he was corrupting the youth and introducing new gods. Luke perhaps suggests that they understood 'Jesus' and 'Resurrection' as two such deities. Perhaps he or they read polytheism in Paul's monotheism, just as Paul is represented as fitting his monotheism to the very altar that was the most eloquent proof of the receptiveness of Athenian polytheism. Probably the evangelist is not exactly contrasting the two, but his story with its repeated emphasis on the novelty of Paul's message and its specific phrase 'new gods' may well be a re-

miniscence of the trial and death of Socrates four centuries and a
half before. Later Christians increasingly adopted Socrates into
their traditions and even confused his trial and Paul's.[44] They also
further unified the scenes in Acts itself by locating the altar of
the Unknown God on the hill of the Areopagus.

In conclusion we may say that though extensive knowledge of
classical Greek literature cannot be attributed to the writer of
Acts, conspicuous facts and phrases of that earlier age lived on
and that he may well have picked them up from contemporary
thought. Beyond that, his work shows a genuine familiarity
with some contemporary Greek localities in which his story is
placed while his language shows in its adaptation of style to
Greek idiom of his time that he was a man of some cultivation,
at home in the speech of the current Greek and not to be reckoned
a mere barbarian or one ill at ease in the speech and civilization
of the far flung area in which the Greek influence had come to
dominate. He is as Jerome inferred for other reasons undoubtedly
the most Hellenic of the evangelists, and in secularity, in language, in approach to literature the nearest to a Greek man of
letters that the early Church provides.

NOTES TO CHAPTER II

1. On the term see J. Jüthner, *Hellenen und Barbaren: aus der Geschichte des
Nationalbewusstseins*, Leipzig, 1923, and T. J. Haarhoff, *The Stranger at the Gate,
aspects of exclusiveness and co-operation in ancient Greece and Rome with some
reference to modern times*, London, 1938, second edition, Oxford, 1948. These
two full titles with the dates and the nationalities (German and South African)
of the authors are worth noting.

2. *Ant. Rom.* ii, 35, 7. Cf. Euripides, *Ion* 8.

3. *Contra Apion.* ii, 41. How long this discrimination lasted is uncertain.
J. G. Winter, *Life and Letters in the Papyri*, 1933, p. 21, follows the older view
that when Caracalla granted Roman citizenship to the whole population of
the Empire the native Egyptians alone were excepted. The evidence of continued use of the poll tax is not so clear as to confirm this inferior status. See
H. I. Bell in *Journal of Roman Studies*, 37, 1947, 17-23. There has been much
recent discussion published on the extension of franchise under Caracalla and
its effect in Egypt. The social inferiority of Egyptians is reflected by the horror
with which an Egyptian 'senator' in the third century is referred to.

4. P. Oxy. xiv, 1681.

5. The data presented by W. L. Knox, *The Acts of the Apostles*, 1948,

Chapter I and Appendix, to refute A. C. Clark's argument for diverse author-ship of the two books, supply, though not so intended, much detailed evidence of the transition to a better vocabulary in the latter half of Acts.

6. C. C. Torrey, *The Composition and Date of Acts,* 1916.

7. *Some Hellenistic Elements in Primitive Christianity.* 1944, pp. 7-22.

8. For likeness of style see Th. Vogel, *Zur Charakteristik des Lukas nach Sprache und Stil,* 2nd edit., 1899, p. 54. For date of 2 Maccabees H. Willrich, *Urkundenfälschung in der hellenistisch-jüdischen Literatur,* 1924, pp. 91-96.

9. Hastings, *Dictionary of the Apostolic Church,* i, 1916, p. 555. On the question of medical language see my *Style and Literary Method of Luke,* 1920.

10. B. G. U. iii, 889.

11. *Definitiones Medicae,* ii (xix. 349 Kühn).

12. *Journal of Biblical Literature,* xliv, 1925, 219 ff; xlv, 1926, 199, *Beginnings of Christianity,* iv, *ad loc.*

13. *Revue Archéologique,* 5ᵉ série X, 1919, pp. 401 ff, copied from Histria IV by Vasile Pârvan, *Analele Academiei Române,* seria ii, tomul xxxviii, 1916, no. 16, pp. 558-593. The Latin begins: *Fines Histrianorum hos esse constitui.* There are actually two copies, both imperfect but supplementary.

14. P. Osl. 26, 14 (5-4 B.C.) ὁλοσκωληκόβρωτος. The shorter term in P. Mich. Zeno, 96, 4; P. Cairo, 59433, 11 and 59728, 5 all of iii/B.C.

15. P. Lond. Inv. 2785, ii, 36 f., ῥήτωρ τῇ δεξί [α...] τὸ ἱμάτιον ἔρρι [ψεν...], published by H. I. Bell in *Archiv für Papyrusforschung,* x, 1935, 5 ff. For earlier discussion of the phrase in Acts, see F. Field, *Notes on the Translation of the New Testament,* 1899, 136, and *Beginnings,* iv, 282; v, 275-277.

16. F. G. Kenyon, *Books and Readers in Ancient Rome,* 1932, p. 36. This was based on an inventory made by C. H. Oldfather in 1922. Kenyon's book appeared in a second edition in 1951 including (pp. 28-36) supplementary data on this subject up to 1945 from L. Giabbani.

17. Roger A. Pack, *The Greek and Latin Literary Texts from Greco-Roman Egypt,* Ann Arbor, 1952.

17a. The untranslatable sobriquet σπερμολόγος used of Paul in Acts 17:18, dilettante, literally seed picker, had been applied by Demosthenes to his opponent Aeschines in his most famous oration, *De corona* 127. Philo, *Leg. ad Gaium* 203 also uses the word, even more plainly in echo of Demosthenes.

18. Cf. Luke 7:11; 7:37; 18:2, 3; 23:19; Acts 8:9; 13:50; 21:29; 25:23.

19. A. C. Clark, *The Acts of the Apostles,* 1933, pp. xlix f. on Acts 20:4.

20. On the urban approach of Luke-Acts see A. Harnack, *The Acts of the Apostles,* Eng. Trans. 1909, pp. 58-63; H. J. Cadbury, *The Making of Luke-Acts,* 1927, pp. 245-249.

21. The number is six not seven (so Demitsas ʽΗ Μακεδονία, Athens, 1896, following Boeckh). In view of the fact that we have a few Thessalonians named in Acts—Jason, Aristarchus, and Secundus and a Berean, Sopater the son of Pyrrhus, it may be worthwhile to note that the inscription begins: 'The politarchs being Sosipater son of Cleopatra and of Lucius Pontius Secundus' (Demitsas 364) while another inscription (*ibid.* 368)—both belong to Thessalonica and the early Roman empire—lists in like manner as the first of five politarchs Aristarchus son of Aristarchus.

22. As an example of an imperial province at the time of Paul's visit may be mentioned Macedonia. It would be ruled by a *legatus Augusti pro praetore* resident at Thessalonica. So was Galatia, and it makes an interesting contrast with the canonical Acts that the *Acta Pauli et Theclae* refer to a trial of Paul at Iconium as before a proconsul (Ramsay, *Church in the Roman Empire*, p. 46). Reference may be made to *Beginnings* v, for the inscriptions of Gallio (pp. 460-464) and Sergius Paulus (pp. 455-459). The latter passage corrects the over eager citation of an inscription to prove the fact and the date of the term of office at Cyprus. But I do not understand how a writer or editor could publish in 1916 a statement, 'There is no other direct evidence that Gallio governed Achaia than St. Luke's statement' (Hastings, *Dictionary of the Apostolic Church*, i, 439). On Gallio compare E. Groag, *Die römischen Reichsbeamten von Achaia bis auf Diokletian*, 1939, col. 32-35.

23. See *Beginnings of Christianity*, v, note xxii, and D. Magie, *Roman Rule in Asia Minor*, 1950, pp. 1298-1301. It is of Ephesus also that the author uses quite correctly another religious term applied especially to cities. It is called 'temple guardian' or sacristan (νεωκόρος) of the goddess Artemis.

24. Similar traits are not lacking in Luke's gospel. Joanna was the wife of Chuzas the steward of Herod (Luke 8 : 2). In the story of the man often called 'the rich young ruler' it is only Luke who calls him ruler (18 : 18), just as it is only Matthew who calls him young (19 : 20).

25. Cf. E. Dinkler, Das Bema zu Korinth, *Marburger Jahrbuch für Kunstwissenschaft*, xiii, 1944, 12-22, with reference to the excavations and illustrations, and a full architectural account by Robert L. Scranton in *Corinth*, vol. i, part iii, Princeton, 1951, pp. 91-109, 124-132. Cf. Oscar Broneer, Corinth: Centre of St. Paul's Missionary Work in Greece, *The Biblical Archaeologist*, xiv, 1951, 78-96, especially 91-92. In an inscription nearby, this tribunal (Greek βῆμα, A.V. judgment seat) is named in Latin *rostra*.

26. The possible identity of the city steward and the aedile I have discussed in *Journal of Biblical Literature* 50, 1931, pp. 42-58; it is accepted by Oscar Broneer, *Biblical Archaeologist*, 14, 1951, p. 94. The offices are not the same, since aedile in Greek is regularly ἀγορανόμος. See D. Magie, *De Romanorum juris publici sacrique vocabulis*, 1905, p. 94. There is a charming imaginative essay by P. N. Harrison, *Erastus and his Ledger*, 1946 (unpublished).

27. The history of the word is somewhat complicated. It is originally probably not Indo-European at all, but perhaps Semitic. It occurs centuries before Acts in a Greek form and probably independently as a Latin noun, as in the Corinthian inscription. Paul's Greek form is probably derived from this later Latin word. On the Corinthian *macellum* see my article in *Journal of Biblical Literature* 53, 1934, pp. 134-141.

28. The words are usually abbreviated on inscriptions and coins and the last word was generally supposed to be *Corinthus*, but in 1941 a first century inscription was found and published by Oscar Broneer in *Hesperia* 10, 388-390, in which the words were spelled out, the last as *Corinthiensis*. See No. 130 in *Corinth* VIII, Part III, Inscriptions 1926-1950, ed. by J. H. Kent.

29. Especially among classical scholars. See E. Norden, *Agnostos Theos*, 1913; E. Meyer, *Ursprung und Anfänge des Christentums*, iii, 1923, 89-108;

W. Schmid, *Philologus*, 95, 1943, pp. 79-120. See also and especially M. Dibelius, 'Paulus auf dem Areopag' in *Sitzungsberichte der Heidelberger Akademie*, 1939, reprinted in his *Aufsätze zur Apostelgeschichte*, 1951, pp. 29-75. N. B. Stonehouse, *The Areopagus Address*, 1949, deals more with the relation of the speech to Christian ideas.

30. Lucian, *Juppiter Tragoedus*, 45, 51.

31. It has even been suggested that the writer knew that he was quoting two poets rather than one and therefore said 'certain ones' instead of 'a certain one', and that he knew that they were Stoic and therefore to win the support of the Stoics in his audience described the poets as 'your own'. But see p. 42.

32. Origen, *Comm. in Johannem*, x, vii (5) § 30, p. 177 Preuschen. He cites the altar too in this connection.

33. The *Beginnings of Christianity*, v, 246-251, and the literature there cited. Other evidence that the words 'In him we live and move and have our being' were regarded as a quotation is found in Athanasius, *De Incarnatione*, 42, (short recension published by Archibald Robertson, London, 1893, p. 64, and reproduced by R. P. Casey, *Studies and Documents* XIV, Part 1, 1946), 'as some writers among them say,' and frequently in Augustine who apparently prefers to attribute this and the passage from the Stoic Aratus to neo-Platonic sources. See F. Chatillon, 'Quidam secundum eos,' Note d'exégèse augustiniene, (*Conf.*, vii, ix. 15), *Revue du moyen âge Latin*, I, 1945, pp. 287-304. He shows that seven times, during some thirty years, Augustine cites the verse Acts 17: 28 in such a way as to omit the quotation from Aratus and to attach the reference to some of yours (not 'your poets') to what precedes.

34. On Epimenides and this quotation see H. Diels, *Fragmente der Vorsokratiker*. In the latest edition, the sixth, edited by Walther Kranz, the reference is vol. i, 1951, pp. 31 f. He notes that the phrase occurred precisely in the prooemium (see above on Aratus) in Hesiod, Epimenides and Callimachus, all three.

35. *Menekrates Zeus und Salmoneus*, 1933, pp. 5-8, 105-108.

36. Rev. 9: 11.

37. *Epist. Aristeae* 16. The double etymology for both forms of the word Zeus occurs in many other authors. See the references in the notes on this passage in Mendelssohn's and Wendland's editions.

38. See K. Lake, 'Your Own Poets,' in *Beginnings of Christianity*, v, 246-251, and the much more cautious and convincing discussion by M. Pohlenz, Ischodad über Act 17: 28' in *Zeitschrift für die neutestamentliche Wissenschaft*, 42, 1949, pp. 101-104, to which I am here indebted.

39. See *Making of Luke-Acts*, p. 159, note. With the indefinite 'someones' compare the indefinite 'somewhere' in citation in Hebrews 4: 4 and five times in 1 Clement, and the double 'someone somewhere' in Hebrews 2: 6, Philo, *De ebrietate* 61. The parallels in pagan writers are abundant though I do not know that they have been collected anywhere. See, for example, W. Langbein, *De Platonis ratione poetas laudandi*. Diss. Jena, 1911, pp. 38 (someone), 54 (somewhere), 38 (plural, poets). A close parallel to Acts (for which I am indebted to A. D. Nock) is Lycurgus, *Leocr.* 132 τῶν ποιητῶν τινες, referring to an unnamed tragedian.

40. The speech at Lystra like that at Athens has the particle καίτοι or καίγε, immediately followed by a case of litotes. It shares the poetical οὐρανόθεν with the speech before Agrippa which by its quotation and other elevated marks of style has also claim to poetical colouring. The criteria or examples of elevated style discussed by G. Rudberg in his essay 'Gedanke und Gefühl, Prolegomena zu einer hellenistischen Stilbetrachtung' (*Symbolae Osloenses Fasc. Supplet.* xiv), 1953, apply well to the speech at Lystra though not so intended. He does emphasize (pp. 13-14) the influence of Aratus as a feature of the higher style, as in the speech at Athens.

41. *Beginnings of Christianity*, v, note xix, and add to the bibliography Jessen in Pauly-Wissowa, Supplement I, 1903, coll. ?8-30, J. A. MacCulloch, *Encyclopaedia of Religion and Ethics*, ix, 1917, p. 180.

42. Notably Norden, *op. cit.* The passage of Jerome is *Comment. in Epist. ad Titum*, i, 12. There are some sixty altar inscriptions from Attica in *Inscriptiones Graecae*, vol. ii and iii, editio minor by J. Kirchner, part 3, 1930, pp. 323-331. They illustrate the use of the dative instead of the genitive and the plural θεοῖς with adjectives. But neither there nor in the further inscriptions published in *Hesperia* does one find any to the unknown god or gods. On this and on all aspects of the scene at Athens one may add to the usual references the discussion in P. Graindor, 'Athènes de Tibère a Trajan' (Université Egyptienne. *Recueil de Travaux*, viii), 1931, pp. 116-126.

43. The successive seasons' labours can be followed in a file of *Hesperia*, the periodical published by the American School of Classical Archaeology in Athens beginning in 1932. The current view of those most competent to judge is that the colonnade or portico where the Areopagus met is the one north-west of the Agora and was called alternately the Stoa Basileios and the Stoa of Zeus Eleutherios. See Ida C. Hill, *The Ancient City of Athens*, 1953, pp. 43-45, based on H. A. Thompson, *Hesperia*, vi, 1937, 64-66.

The possibilities must be left open that the council sometimes met on the hill Areopagus and not in the Agora even in later times, or that Paul spoke on the hill but not to an official group. The inscription of the year 337/6 B.C. found in 1952, in spite of its several references to the council, councillors or council-hall and in spite of the editor's assumptions (*Hesperia* xxi, 1952, p. 358), does not prove that 'Areopagus' alone could be used of the council, or that the phrase 'council (councillors) from Areopagus' implied removal from the hill.

44. ii, 33. The early church paid much more attention to a comparison of Socrates with Christ than to one with Paul. Cf. A. Harnack, *Sokrates und die alte Kirche*, 1900, Giessen, 1901. J. Geffcken, *Sokrates und das alte Christentum*, Heidelberg, 1908. G. M. A. Hanfmann, Socrates and Christ, in *Harvard Studies in Classical Philology*, 60, 1951, 205-233. If Justin Martyr knew the book of Acts, which is doubtful (see below, p. 157) the influence of its account of Paul could be found in his statement (*Apol.*, Appendix 10, 6) that Socrates encouraged men to the recognition through reason of a god unknown to them.

CHAPTER III

ROMAN

Of all the environments which encircle the book of Acts the most universal though in some ways the most superficial is the Roman. It provides the outline, setting and condition of the contemporary civilization, while Greek culture provides more of the intellectual and linguistic and ideological content. Just as the Book of Acts constantly presupposes and often mentions this Roman environment, so that book itself is a first-rate source for an impression of what contemporary life under Rome was like. Not long ago no less a person than the Lord Chief Justice of England, Lord Hewart, made this statement to his fellow classicists:

'It is not often stated, yet perhaps it is the fact, that the best short general picture of the *pax Romana* and all that it meant— good roads and posting, good police, freedom from brigandage and piracy, freedom of movement, toleration and justice is to be found in the experiences written in Greek, of a Jew who happened to be a Roman citizen—that is, in the Acts of the Apostles.'

The basis for this statement is evident to anyone familiar with the book. The explicit references to things Roman and the allusions, often tantalizingly indirect, to other well known Roman matters are abundant. The author, who in his Gospel names the emperors Augustus and Tiberius, in his sequel names Claudius and refers without name to Nero. Of Nero, however, three characteristic contemporary titles are used: Augustus, Caesar, and Lord. Local civil officers of Rome are mentioned quite correctly: proconsuls in senatorial provinces, like Gallio in Achaia and Sergius Paulus in Cyprus, procurators in procuratorial districts like Felix and Festus in Judea, and generals ($\sigma\tau\rho\alpha\tau\eta\gamma o\acute{\iota}$), the usual Greek name for praetors, in the Roman colony of Philippi. Roman soldiers of various ranks are mentioned including beside infantry and cavalry a kind of personnel not elsewhere named or otherwise identified, the δεξιολάβοι.[1] Two centurions, Cornelius and Julius, are mentioned by name. Both were apparently stationed at Caesarea, the headquarters of the Roman military garrison of Judea, and with their names are given the names of their cohorts, the Italian and the Augustan respectively. The first is almost certainly *Cohors II Italica Civium Romanorum.* An inscription in Carnuntum near Vienna which I have seen of an officer of this cohort shows that it was part of the Syrian Army which in A.D. 69 helped win the principate for Vespasian. The other is probably the *Cohors Augusta* whose presence in Syria under Quirinius near the beginning of the century and in Batanea in its second half is also attested by inscriptions. There is likewise conspicuous in the story a higher officer, Claudius Lysias, commander of the Roman cohort in Jerusalem.[2]

Often the references come close to famous persons or places without quite touching them. Certainly two of the most famous Romans under Claudius and Nero were their ministers of state, Seneca the philosopher and Pallas the multimillionaire freedman. Each of them is represented in Acts by a brother. Marcus Annaeus Novatus (later Lucius Junius Gallio Annaeanus), proconsul of Achaia, was brother of Lucius Annaeus Seneca, and Antonius Felix, procurator of Judea, was brother of Marcus Antonius Pallas. As has already been noted, the imperial worship, which almost certainly flourished in several cities of the Empire visited by Paul and which might seem to call for as much notice as, let us say, the magicians in Cyprus and Ephesus or the priest of Zeus-before-the-City at Lystra, is most nearly adumbrated when at Ephesus the Asiarchs are mentioned. They, as we know from other sources, were priests of a provincial league in charge of the worship of the reigning emperor.

Rome's provision for security and transportation mentioned above in the quotation by Lord Hewart, again is only indirectly to be inferred from the story in Acts. The imperial government controlled, if it did not actually own, the merchant marine which brought Egyptian grain to Italy. Two of the three ships

E

in which Paul made his long Roman voyage were ships of Alexandria that may have belonged to this fleet. We learn that one of them had a cargo of grain, and that the other had as its figurehead Castor and Pollux (27: 38; 28: 11).[2a]

Certain episodes of the voyage gain new meaning when we learn what encouragement the emperor Claudius had given to ship owners in this fleet like the ship owner who, by ignoring Paul's advice to spend the winter at Fair Havens in Crete, lost his ship and cargo in a storm. The emperor himself, we are told, had lately undertaken to make good all losses due to storms at sea. In fact, Suetonius says he devised every possible inducement for securing the import of food to Rome even in winter.[3] Puteoli, the harbour at which Paul landed, was the regular terminal for this fleet at the period. Seneca describes graphically the appearance of this harbour when that fleet arrived.[4] Though the road taken by Paul from there to Rome is not mentioned by name but only the stations on it, Forum of Appius and the Three Taverns, we know that it was the ancient Appian Way, already lined near Rome with monuments above ground and columbaria for graves below ground. In Rome itself the author gives us very little local colour. This is an interesting and regrettable contrast to the story at Athens or at Ephesus especially since at Rome the eyewitness seems to be reporting. There is no reference to forums, temples, or other public buildings, not even to the synagogues of Rome, several of which are known to us by name, though Acts mentions merely the Jews.

Beside the Appian Way, many other Roman roads doubtless underlie the numerous itineraries in Acts but are equally unmentioned. Even that brief walk at the very outset of the book from the Mount of Olives to Jerusalem, no longer than a sabbath day's journey, may well have taken place on the Roman road whose steps cut in the stone can still be seen as it goes right over the mountain. When in Macedonia the narrative of Paul and Silas runs, 'And [from Philippi] they took the road through Amphipolis and Apollonia and came to Thessalonica,' (17: 1) we may suppose that they were travelling on the Egnatian Way, one of the main arteries of travel between Rome and the East.

It crossed the Balkan peninsula from Neapolis the harbour of Philippi to Dyrrhachium, whence it was usual for travellers to go by water across the Adriatic Sea to Brundisium and to proceed overland on the Appian Way to Rome. At some time Paul got as far west as Illyricum (Rom. 15 : 19), but on this occasion he did not go past Thessalonica on the rather wild westward continuation of this route but rather turned south to Berea, which was, as it seemed to the Roman Cicero a century before, 'a town off the beaten track,' *oppidum devium*. We have however plenty of evidence elsewhere that Paul also employed the amphibian method of travel which was characteristic of those times. Beside continuous journeys by land, or successive coastwise passages by sea, it was not unusual for travellers to alternate short routes by land with short routes by sea. Among the latter, beside crossings of the Adriatic gulf already mentioned, several others are reported in Acts, a passage of the North East Aegean from Philippi to Troas, and of the North East Mediterranean from Perga to Syrian Antioch (14 : 25-26) or from Patara to Phoenicia (21 : 1-3). Frequently the land and water passages are complete alternatives. Between Corinth and Ephesus, Paul and his friends in the very extensive intercourse revealed in the Epistles used either the direct crossing by water, or the overland route by Macedonia according to the circumstances of the moment, while on one occasion in the brief stage between Troas and Assos the party divided and Paul went by land, not necessarily on foot, and the rest of the party by ship (20 : 13-14).

But to return to the Roman roads, here especially as one can trace them out by modern discovery one experiences the conviction that he is in the very footsteps of St. Paul.[5] It need not be supposed that many roads were exclusively Roman creations. Doubtless these conquerors of the world often took over older routes and we are sure that the Roman routes were in turn taken over by their successors when the Roman Empire fell into decay. But in general we may believe that the principal cities were connected by routes definitely under Roman control, repaired, widened, policed by the provincial government and used for government business. There were fixed lodging places (*mansiones*) at regular distances and between them stations (*stationes*) at which during the day's journey horses were changed. Such marks of Roman use of highways can occasionally be recovered in archaeological remains or identified by references in ancient maps or narratives of journeys. There are also sometimes remains of Roman bridges, but in many ways the most certain identification of Roman routes is the Roman milestone. These heavy stone markers—cylindrical pillars about eight feet high and two feet in diameter with a square base underground—are found frequently all over the area of the ancient Roman Empire.[6] They were repeatedly renewed, often on the same site, until about the fourth century when the Roman government was losing its efficiency. Since the roads remained mostly unchanged in location for all this period the milestones provide substantial and exact evidence of the actual routes used in the days of the Apostles. Other remains of ancient routes exist, but only when confirmed by these unmistakable markers, usually still left by both natives and explorers *in situ*, can a road site be surely identified as Roman.

I have often thought it would be interesting to list and map as completely as possible the surviving Roman milestones on routes probably described in Acts. It would be a difficult task since it would require the mastery of a large body of archaeological and epigraphical literature and perhaps some original research.

Take for example the area of Paul's south Galatian churches, Antioch of Pisidia, Iconium, Lystra and Derbe. While two of these cities were not Romanized until the reign of Claudius as shown by their official names from then on, Claud-Iconium and Claudio-Derbe, both Antioch and Lystra were two of the six colonies in that area established under Augustus and he had provided for their communication. The milestones found along the road connecting these cities bear inscriptions which indicate that the road was called the *Via Augusta*. Although Paul's itinerary in Acts 13-14 included Iconium between the two colonies of Antioch and Lystra, for at least part of the journey he would almost certainly follow the *Via Augusta*.

In many cases scholars have listed only the inscribed stones found; and, though these date sometimes from later than Paul's day, they show often the location of a much earlier road, while the stones without inscription may reach back further than the dated ones. I have mentioned a little earlier the Egnatian Way. Only three stones are listed for this whole stretch of 378 miles all of the same late date of A.D. 217, and only one of the three falls in the part of 100 miles traversed by Paul between Philippi and Thessalonica. But Polybius tells us that in his day, two centuries before Paul, this road was marked throughout with milestones. In the province of Asia on the other hand we have several dated milestones going back that far—to the time of the Gracchi to whom Plutarch assigns the beginning of such activity in road building and road measuring.[7] The next dated stones listed from Asia were actually erected in the time of Paul, i.e. under Claudius and Nero.

I happen to be more familiar with the geography and route problems in Palestine[8] than elsewhere, and Acts provides plenty of material for comparison. Of course it is possible that many of the scenes both here and in the gospel have to do with less conspicuous routes—cross country footpaths such as still connect every two neighbouring hamlets in Palestine. Some at least of the Roman roads marked by milestones were not Roman or at least not so marked until after the events of Acts. But surely several of the events took place on Roman roads. When the Ethiopian eunuch was riding back home from Jerusalem in a chariot he would be likely to use the best roads, even if they traversed desert strips. Philip overtook him in such a place on the road from Jerusalem to Gaza. If as seems likely the first half of that route was identical with the Roman road to the later Roman Eleutheropolis, its location can be fixed by Roman milestones in no less than ten places in about 30 miles. If it was the route via Bethlehem and Hebron eight places can be fixed in the same way in 22 miles.

In the next chapter of Acts we read of Paul's journey from Jerusalem to Damascus and of the vision near the latter city. Now there were many possible ways of making that journey and milestones near Damascus have not been recorded in great numbers, but if Paul went (as I have done) by way of Jericho and Amman the two diverging northern routes from the latter city (then called Philadelphia) are still unusually well marked by milestones, that to the northeast from Philadelphia to Bostra at 39 out of the 53 miles and that to the north to Gerasa at 19 out of the 30 miles.

But of all the journeys in Acts none is more likely to have followed the official Roman route than that described in Acts 23 from Jerusalem to Caesarea. Paul was being removed for safety from Jerusalem under conduct of a heavy guard of nearly five hundred Roman soldiers. Seventy cavalry were to escort him all the way through, four hundred foot soldiers only as far as Antipatris. Now Antipatris lay forty miles northwest of Jerusalem and between them two Roman routes, one going north and then west, and one going west and then north, are at least partly traceable by Roman milestones. The most probable route seems to me to be, however, neither of these but to lie diagonally between the two, not merely because it is more direct but mainly because its terrain through the mountains via the famous upper and lower Beth-horons had commended it for military purposes from the earliest history to modern times. In October A.D. 66, not ten years later than the events in Acts, Cestius Gallus, governor of Syria, advanced from Caesarea to Jerusalem with more than 25,000 men by the route Antipatris, Lydda, Beth-horon and Gibeon and the next month reversed the journey in his ignominious and disastrous defeat.[9]

Now though today an old roadway leaving the Jerusalem-Nablus road about four miles north of the city shows plainly at the fork and is marked on the maps as an ancient road, it was definitely stated in 1917 that no milestones were to be found along it. A few years ago when I was in Jerusalem I felt the challenge of this problem and wishing also to check another Lucan story—the journey to Emmaus—I walked more than once over the whole terrain from the fork near Hanina on the Nablus road to Amwas near the modern Jaffa road, the site of ancient Emmaus or Nicopolis.

I found milestones at three places; first, four miles west of the fork two fragments projecting from a wall at the southern side of the old roadway; second, a full stone lying in the road bed between the two Beth-horons; third, the lower half and base of a Roman milestone lying in a field between Lower Beth-horon and Amwas. It is possible that the last of these and Emmaus itself is not on the shortest route from Beth-horon to Lydda and Antipatris and hence not on the actual route mentioned in Acts. But in the other two instances it was possible for a mere amateur, armed merely with a map and kodak, personally to add two milestones to the list then on record.[10]

Perhaps the largest number of Roman questions in Acts centre in various ways about the matter of Roman citizenship. That topic will at least make a convenient starting point for considering further the Roman background of the book. It is also a subject on which no comprehensive study exists by Roman historians, though an excellent beginning has been made in two books, one by a former student of mine in her doctoral thesis, and one by an Oxford scholar.[11] One of the most influential books on the historical setting of Acts has been Sir William M. Ramsay's *St. Paul the Traveller and the Roman Citizen*. But anyone who looks to it for illumination on the many questions associated with citizenship will be disappointed. The subject was suggested to Professor Ramsay by his teacher, A. M. Fairbairn. 'Roman citizen' was put into the title of the book rather out of *pietas* than as appropriate to the contents.

Let us begin with a dialogue between two citizens reported in the twenty-second chapter of Acts. The time is the sixth decade of the first century of the Christian era, probably early in the reign of Nero. The place is Jerusalem in the barracks overlooking the Temple rebuilt by Herod the Great and connected with its outer court by two pairs of stairs. The barracks themselves had also been rebuilt by Herod and renamed for the famous Mark Antony the Antonia. The Roman procurators used the building as residence, as soldiers' barracks, and as hall of judgment. Some of the Roman or Herodian masonry is still to be identified at the northeast corner of the Haram esh Sherif, or area of the mosque of Omar, including, some have supposed, the large floor slabs of the central area which another Christian writing, the Gospel of John, calls the pavement or Gabbatha, and makes the scene of Jesus' hearing before Pilate.

Of the speakers in the dialogue one is Lysias, a tribune of the Roman cohort. He was stationed by the Roman procurator in the barracks to keep order in the city and Temple. The procurator at this time and for two years longer was one Felix. Of Felix considerable is known from Josephus and from classical sources, but not of Lysias. The other citizen is one Saul, *alias* Paulus, a native of Tarsus in Cilicia, a middle-aged Jew, now a Christian, who has come to Jerusalem again with some funds for the local 'saints'. Something is known of him not only from the present narrative, which is an outline sketch of about a single decade of his Christian life, but from ten letters, more or less, that he wrote in the same decade which are still preserved. Like Lysias, however, he is unmentioned either in Josephus or in ancient classical sources or even in such modern works of reference as Dessau's *Prosopographia Imperii Romani*, or, as we might put it, 'Who's Who in the Roman Empire.'[12]

The reporter is the anonymous author of a vivid anecdotal account of the beginning of Christianity addressed to an unknown Theophilus. His account comprises two volumes, of which the second deals in its last half almost entirely with Paul, and in its last quarter with Paul's experiences as a prisoner in the hands of the law, a series of events of which this scene is the beginning. The reporter was himself a Christian and an admirer of Paul, but not indifferent to secular and political situations or to dramatic effects in his narrative. His accuracy was no doubt dependent on his sources of information. His account in general during this part of his work, whether written in the third person as here, or in the first person as in other passages, appears no less trustworthy than one might expect of an eyewitness.

The circumstances of the conversation were as follows. Paul on his arrival in the city was told by the local Christians—nothing is said of the gift which he brought them nor of their gratitude—that he was suspected of teaching Jews of the dispersion to be renegades to the Law of Moses. Following their advice he undertook to refute the suspicion by an act of voluntary and expensive loyalty to Judaism—connected with some vows being paid in the Temple by four men in whose official rites he associated himself. The suspicion against Paul was not just, but as usually happens, the deliberate effort to dissipate it only made matters worse. Certain Jews of the province of Asia, seeing Paul in the Temple and having seen with him in the city their Gentile fellow countryman, Trophimus of Ephesus, supposed that Paul had introduced him into the temple contrary to the rules of holiness and to the explicit 'No Trespassing for Gentiles' signs which in two languages marked the balustrade within the Court of the Gentiles as the dead line. They raised a hue and cry and dragged Paul into the outer courts. The inner gates were closed, presumably by the Jewish police, while the Roman military tribune policing the Temple from the barracks ran down with some centurions and the companies of soldiers under them and, failing to analyze the exact situation, took Paul into 'protective custody'. On the stairs so great was the violence of the would-be lynchers that the soldiers actually carried Paul. According to our account the first dialogue between Paul and Lysias occurred at this point.

Paul: May I say something to you?

Lysias: Do you speak Greek? What! Are you not the Egyptian who some time ago started a revolt and led into the desert four thousand men of the Assassins (*sicarii*)?

Paul: I am a Jew, a Tarsian of Cilicia, a citizen of no mean city. And I beg you, permit me to speak to the people.

Permission granted, the bilingual Paul turned to his own fellow Jews in the mob below and addressed them in their familiar Aramaic. Though hushed at first they soon burst out again in cries of greater fury and frantic gestures. The tribune, understanding probably neither Paul's speech in Aramaic nor the cries and hostile gestures of the crowd, had Paul taken inside and turned over to a centurion and some soldiers to be examined by scourging. It is here that our principal scene begins.

Paul (to the centurion who stood by at the scourging): Have you the right to scourge a man who is a Roman citizen and uncondemned?

Centurion (going to the tribune Claudius Lysias): What do you intend to do? For this man is a Roman citizen.

Tribune (going to Paul): Tell me, are you a Roman citizen?

Paul: Yes.

Tribune: I myself obtained this citizenship for a great sum of money.

Paul: But I am a citizen by birth.

The last sentence suggests plainly the Latin word *ingenuus*, the technical term for a birthright citizen. For once here I think it cannot be said, 'The Greeks have a word for it.' Was the conversation in Latin, then? Both the speakers turn out to be Roman citizens. We know that as such they were expected to be able to speak Latin, and sometimes suffered penalties if they could not. That does not mean that they regularly did speak in Latin. Even in Rome citizens conversed sometimes in Greek, and in the East that would be a common practice. Perhaps therefore at Jerusalem Paul and Lysias would have talked in the Greek language in which their conversation is reported in Acts.[13]

Now plain as this scene is, it bristles with interesting questions about Roman citizenship. How extensive was it in the East? Had born citizens any advantage over new made citizens? How was citizenship obtained? What relation had it to military service and military advancement? When and how had the tribune probably bought it? How is it likely that it came to be conferred on an ancestor of Paul's? What did it involve for a Jew? How is it related to his citizenship in Tarsus, mentioned just before? What was the evidence that a man was a citizen? What prevented anyone from falsely making such a claim? What real immunities did citizenship offer and were those immunities valid and respected, in Roman provincial, Greek municipal and Jewish civil procedure?

These are some of the questions to which the passage introduces us. The thesis to which I referred deals only with the extension of citizenship under the late republic and early empire (through Augustus). I myself have elsewhere dealt at length with the later vicissitudes of Paul and his appeal to Caesar as related to Roman law[14]. But for answers to many of the questions I scarcely know where to turn. A few observations may be of interest.

As with other questions that we have considered we may begin with names. Every Roman citizen had three names— called *praenomen, nomen,* and *cognomen*—like Marcus Tullius Cicero and Gaius Julius Caesar. The first names were personal and individual, something like our Christian names distinguishing brothers in the same family. But the choice was quite limited, not over fifteen being commonly used at all. Alone they were rather indecisive, yet they are often used alone or at least with some other form of identification. In Acts we have several: Gaius of Thessalonica, Lucius of Cyrene, Marcus, but always in Acts 'John Mark'; and Publius of Malta; and, in Paul's letters Titus,[15] etc. We cannot suppose that these names were always limited to citizens. When used with other names they were abbreviated, usually to one initial,—C, L, M, P, T, etc.

The third name was more often used alone for the individual and in the case before us we have Lysias, a good Greek name, and Paul(l)us, a good Latin name, so employed, almost certainly in each case a *cognomen.* Among other familiar Latin *cognomina* are Agrippa, Aquila, Crispus, Felix, Festus, Niger, Secundus, Tertullus in Acts, and in Paul's letters, Tertius, Quartus, Rufus.

The middle name is the name which associates the individual with the largest number of relatives. It is called *gentilicium* and is connected with *gens,* tribe. It too is sometimes used alone of the individual as for the centurions in Acts, Julius and Cornelius, and very often it is the only name of a Roman woman, e.g. Claudia and Julia in Paul's letters, and Cornelia, Livia, Octavia, etc., in Roman history. Thus each of the three names is used of different individuals as the single name, as indeed it is of Roman emperors with *praenomina* like Tiberius and Titus, with *nomina* like Claudius, and with *cognomina* like Nero, not to mention nicknames like Caligula or formal titles like Augustus. Only their great predecessor was indifferently called by each of three, Gaius or Julius or Caesar. Nowhere in the New Testament are all three names given for an individual though occasionally in Acts we have the last two, especially of Roman officials as Pontius Pilatus, Sergius Paulus, Porcius Festus, perhaps also Titius Justus, and in the case of our military tribune when his letter is quoted, Claudius Lysias. We know that the Agrippa in Acts was Marcus Julius Agrippa and that after adoption Gallio was Lucius Junius Gallio. Strangely enough Paul's name could be either *praenomen* or *cognomen*. We are more familiar with the latter use as in Lucius Aemilius Paulus, the Roman victor at Pydna, and in L. Sergius Paulus, Paul's own contemporary. But an associate of the latter was called Paullus Fabius Persicus, and a Paullus Fabius Maximus is mentioned in inscriptions in Rome and in Cyprus. As a *praenomen*, Paullus was not unusual in the East.

This practice of using last names for first names—not unlike the use of surnames for Christian names in our own customs—is only one of the signs of the breakdown of the old three name system of the republican period. Another custom which began in the East and spread throughout the Empire was the use of an extra name, which the Latin called a *signum* and we might call—but with no unfavourable connotation—an *alias*. The ancients indicated the connexion by the expression 'who was also' (*qui et = ὁ καὶ*, e.g. 'Hermes who was also Mercurius') which is precisely found in the passage in Acts (13 : 8) where we read 'Saul who was also Paul'. This idiomatic feature of his name makes up in part for our want of knowledge of two of his technical Roman names.

As a single Roman name is no evidence of Roman citizenship so a single non-Roman name is no evidence of the lack of it. Though called Saul in the early part of Acts, Paul was none the less a Roman already. So was the tribune when called Lysias. Indeed most Greeks when franchised kept their previous name as a *cognomen*, or else the non-Roman name remained with them as an alternative. Silas, Paul's associate, may be an example. At least it is implied in Acts 16 : 37 that he was a Roman and Paul in his epistles indicates that his Latin name was Silvanus. Perhaps if writing his full name it would have been expressed as:

'―― ―― Silvanus, alias Silas.' We know another Silas of this century, in fact a king, who set up his monument at Edessa in A.D. 78 and who gives his name as Gaius Julius Samsigeramus, alias Silas. According to Ramsay's conjecture the Apostle's full name would be Gaius Julius Paulus, alias Saul.

Now the triple Roman name was *prima facie* evidence of Roman citizenship. It was only insecure evidence as it could easily be assumed, and to avoid misuse the unauthorized assumption of a Roman name was more than once forbidden. The emperor Claudius, we read in Suetonius, forbade men of the status of *peregrini* to employ Roman names, at least the *gentilicia*. But, as Suetonius continues, the actual false claiming of citizenship was even more serious. 'Those who illegally assumed Roman citizenship he had executed by the lictor's axe in the Campus Esquilinus.'[16] Epictetus reminds the philosopher who falsely bears the name of Stoic how severely those are punished who falsely claim Roman citizenship.[17]

How could a soldier in Jerusalem or Philippi know whether Paul in claiming exemption from scourging as a Roman citizen was doing so falsely or truly? Did Paul carry a passport as evidence? The diploma of a discharged soldier, a portable certificate of which we know,[18] would serve in the veteran's case since he secured citizenship upon retirement from the army, but Paul was born a citizen. A birth certificate would have the same value. Actual examples of such birth certificates of Roman citizens have lately been coming to light. In Egypt they were not Greek papyri, but were waxed tablets written in Latin, certified copies of records posted at Alexandria within thirty days of the child's birth. They were held by the citizen himself and were probably used as an indication of his age, his identity, his relationship, his legal heirship to his father's estate and his privileges of Roman citizenship. We have a few references in literature also to the use of birth certificates in the second century, to prove age in court or to prove citizenship. It is true that the life of Marcus Aurelius in the Augustan History speaks as though Marcus Aurelius had been the first to establish the use of public tablets in the provinces in order that if any one born in the provinces had to prove himself a free man he might secure evidence from that source. But something of the sort was almost certainly practised earlier.[19]

Such certificates were of course only copies of official records. They referred to these, and their own genuineness could in the last resort be tested by them. There was presumably a complete roster at Rome and we have lately learned also of records in the provinces. We know the official title of the registrar of births in both instances. Especially interesting is an inscription of the year A.D. 6 lately found by Italian excavators at Cyrene in northern Africa. The local government had a list of the 215 Roman citizens in the province available for jury duty. These lists would be revised at each census and the local as well as complete lists would contain each individual's name. The local citizens of a province or a district constituted a Roman court in the district. Thus in Asia as the proconsul went from city to city to decide cases the Roman citizens in the district were assessors at the court over which the proconsul himself presided. This citizen assembly was called in Latin *conventus*, in Greek ἀγοραῖος, that is, ἡ ἀγοραῖος ἡμέρα. The latter word is used in the story in Acts after the riot at Ephesus where the town clerk, wishing to refer the dispute to legal procedure, reminds the populace that there are such things as proconsuls[20] and citizen assemblies (19: 38).

A census is twice mentioned in Luke's writings (Luke 2: 1; Acts 5: 37) though he once implies that it was for more than Roman citizens. In Egypt, at least in the time of Paul, there was a regular census every fourteen years. It would certainly include Roman citizens. Occassionally local censuses were taken of the whole population as in Judea under Quirinius in A.D. 6, after the death of Herod Archelaus. But we have no evidence of a worldwide census of all the population quite as early as Luke's Gospel suggests. At Cyrene a few years after the birth of Jesus they had no lists of others than Romans. So at least some scholars believe, though others take the view that the existence of lists of non-Romans is implied in the Cyrene edicts.[21] At any rate it is the total of Roman citizens eligible for jury duty there which is given.

The chronological difficulties involved in the two references to a census in Luke-Acts are particularly unfortunate.[22] If in either or both of them the author refers to a census taken in Syria in A.D. 6-7 when Judea was united to that province under the governor P. Sulpicius Quirinius, special interest for us attaches to a Latin funerary inscription published in 1674 from a stone since lost.[23] In it the deceased tells of having taken for Quirinius a census of the people of Apamea, a city on the Orontes in Syria, and gives the total as 117,000. This figure is evidently not of Roman citizens but of all the free people of the city.

Another example of local evidence of citizenship, and one of particular interest here because it has to do with Tarsus, is a set of decrees awarding citizenship and other privileges to a certain naval captain of Octavian, Seleucus of Rhosus in Syria, or rather on the border of Cilicia and Syria. It is a copy of a decree recorded on a stele at the Capitol in Rome but it provides that it should be copied in the public records not only at Rhosus, the citizen's home, but also at the neighbouring metropolis of Tarsus, at Antioch and elsewhere.[24] The date of the award is 41 B.C., perhaps no earlier than the acquisition of citizenship by the Apostle's forbears. In which case they and Seleucus of Rhosus would have appeared on the same Tarsus list.

How citizenship came to Paul's family is of course a matter of conjecture. It is usually supposed that they were Jewish slaves taken captive in Palestine by Pompey in 63 B.C. and deported to Tarsus, and there freed. Jewish freedmen were found in other parts of the empire. Indeed Acts itself (6:9) mentions a Synagogue of Freedmen in Jerusalem, and that in close association with Jews from Cilicia. Most probably a descendant of freedmen would also worship in such a synagogue. The author of Acts in his description of Stephen's opponents very likely mentions the group to which Paul belonged as well as Paul himself. There is more evidence at Rome of Jewish freedmen. In the reign of Tiberius Jewish and Egyptian freedmen to the number of 4,000 were banished by the Senate to Sardinia. Some of these were possibly Gentile freedmen who had become Jews, but others like

Paul's ancestors may well have been not proselytes but of Jewish descent.

Citizenship by emancipation seems at first sight more certain in the case of Claudius Lysias. He had bought it himself, in his own lifetime. If this means that having been the slave of a Roman citizen he had bought his own liberty, as indeed slaves often did, then the large price he speaks of was paid to his master. We know something of the prices paid for slaves or by them for their own remission. The ordinary prices run from 200 to 600 or 1000 drachmae or denarii, i.e. the one time equivalent of about $40 to $120 or $200, but fancy prices are quoted by Pliny the Elder running into the highest figures. Of course often slaves were freed at less than their value or indeed for nothing by their generous masters. The words of Claudius Lysias exclude this from his case. 'With a great sum bought I this freedom.'

Slave manumission however was not the principal method of acquiring Roman citizenship. Free residents of the Roman empire, i.e. *peregrini*, also came into possession of its privileges and that too in many ways. The Roman army was one medium of the extension. Under the Republic the regular legions had always consisted of Roman citizens. That meant Italians, but in the Civil Wars, with the unusual demand for recruits, provincials were enrolled, and in order to continue the requirement they were given citizenship by the general upon their entry into service. Antony must have thus granted citizenship to thousands in the Eastern provinces before his defeat at Actium. The emperors followed the same policy. The auxiliary forces of the army were, except for their officers, not Roman citizens, but upon their discharge they too were given the franchise. In these two ways nearly twenty thousand persons a year may have become Roman citizens. Paul's ancestors, however, probably did not acquire citizenship in this way. We know that Jews were not abundant in the auxiliary forces, and those that were already citizens were exempted from military service.

Another form of extension was in the colony. The planting of colonies outside of Italy was a policy begun by Julius Caesar and continued by his successors. An existing community was reorganized, by the settlement in it of Roman citizens and by giving to it a Roman form of government. But the local natives were also in time made Roman citizens. Such a colony served several purposes. It provided land and a home to the large numbers of veterans retired from the army. It established in areas needing defence or in danger of revolt a loyal city or group of cities. When suitably located it fostered trade and occupation for citizens. A good many colonies are mentioned in Acts, though the author calls attention to that status only in one of the oldest of them, Philippi. This and Corinth were both made colonies by Julius Caesar. The former consisted largely of veterans, the latter of freedmen. Colonies of Augustus include Syracuse in Sicily, Troas in Asia, and Pisidian Antioch and Lystra, established for defence against the Pisidian tribes. Ptolemais in Syria and Iconium[25] in Galatia were each made a colony by Claudius. These are I think all of the colonies mentioned in Acts. Tarsus however was as we said still a Greek city and unless Paul's ancestors had previously lived elsewhere they could not have acquired citizenship in this way.

Finally we have the granting of citizenship to individuals— free *peregrini* living within the Empire. Just how extensively this was done we have no way of knowing, but it had been practised for generations and may be the method by which both Paul's forbears and Lysias came to be citizens. I have already cited the instance of Seleucus of Syrian Rhosus. He received citizenship in 41 B.C. for signal service to the state, or at least to the cause of Octavian who thus rewarded him. To other persons citizenship was granted in the hope of securing their support. Julius Caesar had thus given citizenship to many political leaders and nobles in Gaul and Spain[26] and to royal families or native politicians in the East. Antipater, the ancestor of all the Herods, had thus secured civic status for all his house. Men of letters also were sometimes thus individually rewarded. But was Paul's ancestor any of these? If not, this still may quite possibly have been the process by which his family's citizenship began. It was given for less substantial reasons and sometimes for gain.

Cicero makes exactly that charge against Antony.[27] He sold

F

kingship, citizenship and exemption for money. The ugly charge recurs a century later. Dio Cassius says that in the reign of Claudius citizenship was sold for large sums under Messalina and the Emperor's freedmen but that later a man could get it for a mere bauble.[28] Claudius Lysias may well have belonged to the earlier creations of the period. His name Claudius fits, because the *gentilicium* of newly made citizens and their descendants is usually that of the general or dictator under whom soldiers receive citizenship at enlistment or discharge, under whom colonies are founded, or through whom individuals receive the franchise. The fiction in all these cases was authorization by the Senate or Roman people but the new citizen received the imperator's name. The principal class of citizens to receive other *gentilicia* would be the freed slaves of citizens of other *gentes*. There is the greatest probability that the Julius of one centurion in Acts goes back to either Gaius Caesar or Augustus, the Cornelius of another centurion may revert still earlier to Sulla, and the Claudius of the tribune Lysias to the emperors Tiberius or Claudius. As for Paul, it is a handicap to the solution of our problem that his middle or gentilic Roman name is not known to us. The name might suggest with a good deal of probability the time if not the circumstances under which his Tarsian Jewish family came on to the list of Roman citizens.

If we turn now from the acquisition of citizenship to more general consideration of its extent and value, we must content ourselves with a few remarks. Something has already been said to suggest the abundance of citizens in the East. There were Italians resident abroad as traders or officials, there were the citizens in the army, and in the colonies. There were freedmen and individual citizens who had received the franchise. Beside the freedmen in Jerusalem mentioned in Acts, Romans there, i.e. citizens, are mentioned among the people at Pentecost. The census lists give us some information about the numbers in the early Empire. By comparing the numbers we can estimate the speed by which the franchise was extended in the first century of the Empire. I shall quote in round numbers the totals for the beginning and end of the reign of Augustus, both taken from his own official *Res Gestae* and one total for a later period.

In 28 B.C. the citizens numbered just over four million, at A.D. 14 very nearly five million, in A.D. 47 very nearly six million.[29]

Although therefore citizenship was not so select as formerly, it was still highly prized. The advantages of citizenship were numerous. Very few citizens abroad would be likely to return to Rome and actually vote there, though they had that privilege. They could of course run for office, and after one or more generations new made citizenship acquired additional advantages. The Book of Acts suggests certain legal advantages—immunity from scourging and the right of appeal to Rome. But within what limitations these were either guaranteed or actually observed is much more difficult for us to learn than might be suspected of such apparently simple problems.

That exemption from corporal punishment and other privileges of Romans were sometimes ignored we know from the complaints of Cicero. We may wonder why though in Jerusalem Paul's claim of citizenship protected him from a kind of third degree examination, it did not do so on other occasions. Paul says he was thrice beaten with rods (2 Cor. 11 : 25), apparently the official rods of Roman lictors, and Acts itself tells us of one such instance, at Philippi, in which only after it was over did the Roman magistrates pay any attention to the claim of citizenship.

In one instance we recall that even non-Romans could inflict summary execution upon a Roman citizen. We have made mention of the strict exclusion by Jewish ritual of foreigners from the inner courts of the Jerusalem Temple. According to Josephus the Romans ratified this prohibition and permitted the Jews to put to death any who passed the balustrade, even were he a Roman.[30] No doubt the mob that assailed Paul was not afraid of legal technicalities but the charge of defiling the Temple was one in which the claim of Roman citizenship would have been of little use, even at a formal and orderly meeting of the sanhedrin. Though the Book of Acts does not make the point clear, it does mention the precise charge against Paul, which, if substantiated, alone could have cancelled the citizen's immunity from summary punishment. In like manner Acts does not make it clear that in appealing from the procurator's jurisdiction to Caesar's Paul was taking advantage of a privilege limited only to citizens. Shall we suppose that the ancient reader could be expected to recognize the connection? Or that the author himself fully recognized it?

Other legal advantages accrued in the realm of property[31] and inheritance and, naturally, social advantages. The marriage of a citizen and a non-citizen was illegal. I recall seeing in Vienna a copy of an epitaph there which reads, 'Publius Titius Finitus aged forty made this in his life time for himself and for Jucunda, the daughter of a citizen, his wife.' It has been supposed that in the portraits of the family sculptured on the stone Publius is proudly holding his own citizenship papers. The privileges of Roman citizens are well indicated for Rome and the provinces about 50 B.C. in Cicero's orations and for Egypt in A.D. 150 in the financial code called the 'Gnomon of Idios Logos'. For the events of Acts about halfway between these dates we can easily conjecture the advantages. Even within citizenship there were further differences. The conversation in Acts suggests a difference between newly made and born citizens, for one can hardly suppose that Paul is merely boasting of the comparative cheapness of his own birth-right citizenship.

The freedman, for example, was far from being on a par with the hereditary citizen.[32] He was scorned by the latter, especially at Rome, and both he and his son were legally debarred from membership in the Senate or even in the equestrian class. His name was always telltale, particularly since his former master's name must also be given in official documents. His own earlier name was retained as *cognomen* and whether Greek like Lysias or even a common Latin slave name like Felix it was strongly suggestive of servile origin. The custom of inserting the father's name betrayed free or slave origin a generation earlier. Thus the prestige of Romans born of Romans was preserved. We can understand therefore why one paragraph of the Idios Logos required: 'From those Egyptians who after the death of their fathers enrolled their fathers as Romans a fourth part of the estate is confiscated' (§ 43).

In the case of a military career, if that was the ambition of Claudius Lysias, the advantages of Roman citizenship can easily be understood and the motives which led him to pay a large sum for it. For a non-citizen to buy citizenship probably involved bribery and was as illegal as in modern times; but it was no less possible. One wonders if Lysias would openly boast of having done so.[33] Citizenship was necessary for entering the lowest rank in the regular army and for being an officer, apparently even of the lower grade, in the auxiliaries, whether in an infantry cohort or in a cavalry *ala*. Certainly without it Claudius Lysias could never have become, as he was, a tribune in the auxiliaries stationed in Palestine. Even with citizenship a man rarely rose so far from the ranks.[34] This position not only brought in much better pay—in the regular legions a centurion got more than sixteen times as much as the 'private' (*miles gregarius*)—it was the beginning of an equestrian career. The social reward of being within striking distance of the equestrian order or probably on a level with the members of the town council of a municipality was not inconsiderable. If the ambition of Claudius Lysias was political a term of military service as tribune of a cohort was a prerequisite of the whole *cursus honorum*, and the post was usually filled by young men beginning the equestrian *cursus*. That at least was the case after the middle of the first century, but earlier we have evidence that the *praefecti cohortis* or *alae* like the *tribuni legionis* were veteran centurions from the legions, especially the *primipili*. Since the scene in Acts belongs neither early or late in the first century the exact standing of Claudius Lysias is·beset with peculiar uncertainty.

Roman citizenship was not however without its responsibilities. Like newly made American citizens today, they could be debarred for ignorance of the language of their new fatherland. There were taxes for which Roman citizens were alone responsible, especially a five per cent inheritance tax. I suppose that theoretically citizens were subject to *dilectus*, or draft for military service, though that was sometimes met in the case of Jews by a general rule of exemption. The Jewish sabbath and dietary laws made it difficult to integrate them in any effective military unit. Particularly were the religion and morals of citizens subject to regulation. Apparently much of the objection to foreign religions at Rome was due to the incursions which they made upon freedmen and citizens. The Jews were only intermittently and irregularly dealt with at Rome. Such severity as was practised against them under Claudius, as well as earlier, beginning perhaps as long before as 139 B.C., was due to fear of their proselytizing in the citizen class. This thought gives a good deal of meaning to the description in Acts of the charge against Paul and Silas in Philippi (16 : 20-21). That it was a colony the historian has already mentioned, but he represents the complainants as saying: 'These men . . . are Jews and are announcing customs which it is illegal for us to accept or to practise, seeing we are Romans.' The incurable missionary impulse of early Christianity very likely brought down upon it at Rome or wherever else Roman citizens were involved the strong hand of Rome, while its likeness to Judaism, indistinguishable to an outsider, inevitably involved Jews in the same disaster—perhaps almost contemporaneously at Rome, Corinth, and Alexandria.

Of the relation of citizenship to Judaism on the one hand and to local citizenship on the other our fullest information comes from Alexandria. That city also had its own form of citizenship, so that in Egypt a registration of persons would include as different classes Egyptians, Alexandrian citizens, Romans, freedmen and non-residents. Probably no Egyptian was admitted to Roman citizenship without being first an Alexandrian citizen. Whether for others Roman citizenship carried Alexandrian citizenship with it is uncertain. That is one of the many questions raised by the letter of Claudius in which he tells Gentile citizens not to deny the Jews their rights as citizens of Alexandria and perhaps other Jews not to aspire to Alexandrian citizenship which they did not possess.[35] Certainly Josephus would lead us to suppose that in Alexandria and indeed in many other of the Greek cities in the East, Jews had local citizenship.

But was it possible to have both Roman and local citizenship?[36] That depends upon the date. It was not possible in the earlier days, as Cicero makes plain in his *Pro Balbo* 28: *Duarum civitatum civis noster esse iure civili nemo potest*. In his *Laws* Cicero seems to admit dual citizenship only from the point of view of sentiment. Probably the way for it had been prepared in the Greek cities of the East by what was called isopolity. Members of a league of cities must have retained local citizenship as well, and upon individuals honorary citizenship of other cities was conferred. The Roman government could not but come to a similar practice. The wide extension of citizenship, which as the census figures show had doubled the numbers in Cicero's lifetime and which especially had extended it to well established cities outside of Italy, required a new attitude to dual citizenship. Incompatibility, as it is called, gave place to compatibility. The edicts of Augustus at Cyrene show the process in development. The question took this form: Were citizens of Cyrene who were also citizens of Rome liable to the services required by both cities? Evidently this would put upon some a double burden. On the other hand it would be manifestly hard on the local government if all Roman citizens in residence and belonging to it, often its wealthiest and ablest citizens, could not be called upon for local services. Augustus recognizes the double citizenship and the double responsibility. In a limited number of specially favoured cases, however, an immunity from local requirements was explicitly conferred along with Roman citizenship. Such immunity is mentioned in the Cyrenian decree. It had been conferred earlier on Seleucus of Rhosus and Antipater of Judea. But it is a provision made in the light of dual citizenship and that latter principle therefore was thoroughly established when about A.D. 55 the Apostle Paul is represented as saying in one context, 'I am a Roman, I was born so'; and in another, 'I am a Jew of Tarsus, a citizen of no mean city.'

The attitude to Rome implied in this single question of citizenship may well be latent in other parts of the book.[37] For even among freedom loving peoples of the East respect for Rome was growing and an appreciation of what seemed to be its genius and its destiny to assimilate into a single citizenship the whole world. To this process the wise leadership of the Empire and the willing understanding and admiration of its subjects were already leading. We are concerned with two of the latter, with Paul and his biographer. As a Christian Paul anticipates the universalism of the secular trend when he speaks of his citizenship as in heaven, and so Tertullian understands him,[38] or when he says, 'Here there cannot be Greek and Jew, circumcised and uncircumcised, barbarian, Scythian, slave and free,' much as an anonymous writer says 'neither Syrian nor Greek nor barbarian nor any other people shall put the neck under Rome's yoke.'[39]

So Paul's biographer, when he speaks repeatedly of the inhabited world, when he uses for the Emperor the cementing concept of king, is anticipating the process by which the Empire was to unite mankind until Greek and Roman would be synonyms and barbarian would scarcely be applicable anywhere in the civilized world but only to the new external enemies of Rome itself. One can scarcely believe that in mentioning so favourably the Asiarchs, though he does not hint at their idolatrous connexion with the religious cult of Rome and the Emperor, he was ignorant that they represented the intense loyalty of Asian provincials to the Empire, as the imperial officials that he mentions elsewhere are symbolic of the unifying and beneficent influence for law and peace which actively fostered that loyalty. If he does not foresee all the implications of the Empire of his day, the coming conflict between church and state, between what Augustine later calls indifferently the Roman city, the earthly city or the world (*civitas Romana, civitas terrena, orbis terrarum*) and the City of God (*civitas dei*), it is simply because he is true to the perspective of his own time.

NOTES TO CHAPTER III

1. See W. Bauer, *Griechisch-deutsches Wörterbuch, s.v.*

2. On the Roman army as background of the Book of Acts see T. R. S. Broughton in *Beginnings of Christianity*, v, 427-445.

2a. F. J. Dölger, the veteran student of this secular background of early

Christianity published in 1950 an article on 'Dioskuroi'. Das Reiseschiff des Apostels Paulus und seine Schutzgötter, *Antike und Christentum*, vi. 276–285.

3. *Claudius* 18, 2. By the gift of citizenship (see below) the Emperor induced shipbuilders to supply new ships for this trade. Gaius, *Inst.* i, 32 c.

4. *Ep.* 77.

5. This impression was already suggested by the title of Sir William M. Ramsay's *St. Paul the Traveller and the Roman Citizen*, 1896. See also the attractive later books, H. V. Morton, *In the Steps of St. Paul*, 1936, and R. Martin Pope, *On Roman Roads with St. Paul*, 1939.

6. See the article 'miliarium' by K. Schneider in Pauly-Wissowa, Supplementband vi.

7. *C. Gracchus*, 7, 2.

8. The discussion in the text is based on P. Thomsen, Die römischen Meilensteine der Provinzen Syria, Arabia und Palestina (with map) in *Zeitschrift des Deutschen Palästina-Vereins*, 40, 1917, pp. 1–103, with additions noted in the *Quarterly of the Department of Antiquities of Palestine*, 12, 1946, 96–102. For Palestine west of the Jordan more complete, as more recent, is M. Avi-Yonah, *Map of Roman Palestine*, Second Edition, 1940.

9. Josephus, *B.J.* II, xix, 1 (515–516) and 8–9 (546–555). The road is that described *ibid.* II, xii, 2 (228) as the public road.

10. For this road see now Avi-Yonah, *op. cit.*, p. 43, number (6) A.

11. Charlotte E. Goodfellow, *Roman Citizenship, A Study of Its Territorial and Numerical Expansion from the Earliest Times to the Death of Augustus*, 1935. A. N. Sherwin-White, *The Roman Citizenship*, 1939. Further literature on the subject is extensive. I mention only the review of Sherwin-White by A. Momigliano in the *Journal of Roman Studies*, 31, 1941, pp. 158–165.

12. By E. Klebs, H. Dessau and P. von Rohden, 3 vols., 1897–1898. The second edition now in progress, does include Claudius Lysias.

13. On the use or requirement of Latin, cf. C. S. Walton in *Journal of Roman Studies*, 19, 1929, pp. 40 f.

14. *Beginnings of Christianity*, v, 297–338.

15. An impression of the relative frequency of these praenomina may be gained by noting their proportion in a total of over 2,500 Latin names in *Corpus Inscriptionum Latinarum*, vol. i (G. D. Chase, *The Origin of Roman Praenomina*, Harvard Ph.D. thesis, 1897, p. 130). Lucius and Gaius each account for over 20 per cent, Marcus for over 15, Publius for 9, Titus for 3.

16. *Claudius* 25, 3.

17. Arrian, *Ench.* III, 24, 41.

18. In 1936, volume 16 of the *Corpus Inscriptionum Latinarum* was published containing 157 *diplomata militaria*. More have been published since. They are as the name implies folded double, like a diptych. They are written on bronze and refer to official lists of veterans discharged and enfranchised, kept at the Capitol in Rome. The earliest of them are dated contemporary with the events in Acts. Some evidence suggests that this reward of veterans from the auxilia was begun under Claudius.

19. *Scriptores Historiae Augustae*, M. Antonius, 9, 7f. On birth certificates compare Apuleius, *Apologia* 89, with the notes to it in H. E. Butler and A. S. Owen's edition, 1914, p. 158.

20. The reference to proconsuls would not always be reassuring. As Cicero shows, they had not a reputation for defending the economic interests of the provincials of Asia. At the time of Paul's visit to Ephesus at least the three copies known to us in Greek or Latin were to be seen about the city of a decree of the recent proconsul Paullus Fabius Persicus. In it he speaks, like the actors in the story of Acts, with respect for the prestige of the goddess and with insistence that none of the income shall be tampered with. See F. K. Dörner, *Der Erlass des Statthalters von Asia Paullus Fabius Persicus*, Greifswald, 1935.

21. On the Cyrene edicts, for example, A. Premerstein in *Zeitschrift der Savigny-Stiftung*, 48, 1928, Rom. Abteilung, pp. 448 ff., takes the view that lists of non-Romans were not available, while L. R. Taylor in *American Journal of Philology*, 54, 1933, 120-133, believes the opposite. See in general F. de Visscher, *Les Édits d'Auguste découverts à Cyrène*, Louvain, 1940. The inscriptions were first published by G. Oliviero in 1927.

22. The problem is complicated and the literature is abundant and contradictory. Against the A.D. 6-7 date for the census of Luke 2 : 1, is the fact that the author seems to place the birth of Jesus before the death of Herod the Great in 4 B.C. Against that date for the census of Acts 5 : 37 is the fact that the author places the rise of Judas of Galilee *after* the episode of Theudas, which in turn is later than the situation in Acts where it is mentioned. Even the generally accepted statement of Josephus, *Antiq.*, 18. 2, 1, that the census in which Judas was active occurred in the thirty-seventh year after Actium (A.D. 6-7) has been challenged by W. Lodder, *Die Schätzung des Quirinius bei Flavius Josephus*, 1930.

23. T. Mommsen in *Ephemeris Epigraphica*, iv, 1881, 537-542. Cf. F. Cumont, The Population of Syria, *Journal of Roman Studies*, 24, 1934, 187-190.

24. P. Roussel, 'Un Syrien au service de Rome et d'Auguste,' *Syria*, xv, 1934, 33-74. This is merely the *editio princeps* in a large bibliography.

25. Whether Iconium of Galatia was a colony of Claudius or of Hadrian is not agreed. See Pauly-Wissowa, *s.v.* Colonia (Kornemann) and Ikonion (Ruge) and Vincent M. Scramuzza, *The Emperor Claudius*, 1940, p. 283.

26. A grant by the father of Pompey the Great to some Spanish cavalry as early as 89 B.C. is recorded in Dessau, *Inscriptiones Latinae Selectae*, 8888.

27. *Philipp.*V, iv, 11.

28. 60, 17, 6-8. But Dio had just said (60, 17, 4) that Claudius had withheld or withdrawn citizenship from individuals without knowledge of Latin. Cf. Suetonius, *Claudius* 16, 2. The policy of Claudius as to extending citizenship both to individuals and to whole communities is shown to us by the sources in a somewhat contradictory light. It is ably analyzed by Sherwin-White, *op. cit.* chap. viii, pp. 181-193 and by Vincent M. Scramuzza, *The Emperor Claudius*, 1940, chapter vii. The policy of Claudius appears to have been neither lavish nor ultra conservative.

29. Tacitus, *Ann.* xi, 25, 5. The figures for the earlier years are more certain since they come from the *Res Gestae* of Augustus. Cf. Goodfellow, *op. cit.*, p. 27.

30. Josephus, *B.J.*, vi, 126.

31. One of the volumes of papyri contains as its only non-literary item two fragmentary copies of a census return of a landowner in Oxyrhynchus in

Egypt who declared that he and his sons had been presented with Roman citizenship by the emperor Claudius in the year A.D. 45-46. Unfortunately we cannot tell what this information had to do with his privileges as part owner of two houses: *PSI* xi, 1183, *idem professus se et filios civitate donatos esse ab Ti. Claudio Caesare Aug. Germanico imp. Ti. Plautio Silvano Aeliano Tauro Statilio Corvino cos.*

32. The legal disabilities of the freedman (*libertus, libertinus*) compared with the free born (*ingenuus*) had been defined at least in part in the reign of Augustus by a lex Junia,—hence the term *Latinus Junianus.* On all these matters see A. M. Duff, *Freedmen in the Early Roman Empire*, 1928.

33. Citizenship of Greek cities like that of Rome was sometimes bought for money. This practice is mentioned more often in our sources, and apparently without censure. The exceptions are when the city sold its rights without discriminating among purchasers, or charged too little for it (a mina) as at Phaselis in Lycia or too much (500 drachmae) as at Tarsus of Cilicia. See respectively Macarius 8, 26, and Dio Chrysostom 34, 23, and in general L, Robert, Sur un dicton relatif à Phasélis. La vente du droit de cité, *Hellenica* I. 1940, pp. 37-42.

34. In the auxilia the term *praefectus* seems to have been generally used in place of *tribunus* for men of this rank except for a special group of cohorts in which, at least in the time of our story, freedmen or *peregrini* were not enrolled, but only Roman citizens, to whom the words *voluntarii* or *ingenui* were applied. So G. L. Cheesman, *The Auxilia of the Roman Imperial Army*, 1914, pp. 65-67. For the whole subject see, beside Cheesman and Broughton, *loc. cit.* M. Durry, *Les cohortes prétoriennes*, Paris, 1938, and C. G. Starr, Jr., *The Roman Imperial Navy*, 1941.

35. H. I. Bell, *Jews and Christians in Egypt*, 1924. But it is difficult to see how Jews could be citizens without being renegades to their religion like Tiberius Alexander, nephew of Philo and prefect of Egypt. Equally insecure, I think, is the view of W. W. Tarn, *Hellenistic Civilization*, 1927, p. 176 f. (Third edit. 1952, p. 221 f.) that the Jew had a virtual citizenship, or right to citizenship, which he could claim when or if he adopted Gentile ways.

36. As an answer to this question my colleague Mason Hammond prepared an informative article entitled 'Germana Patria', published in *Harvard Studies in Classical Philology*, 60, 1951, pp. 147-174. He shows the precedents which prepared the way in both East and West for dual citizenship under the Empire.

37. And Rome's contribution to history is perhaps best revealed in the same question. Momigliano, *loc. cit.*, p. 158, says: 'If there is any royal road to the essential values of Roman history it is in the study of Roman citizenship. The system of civil rights shows the distance between Rome and the Oriental empires, the Hellenistic monarchies, and the Greek city states, and it indicates the points of contact between the ways of Rome and those of the Church: St. Paul's citizenship remains a landmark.'

38. Phil. 3 : 20 πολίτευμα; Tertullian, *Adv. Marcionem* iii, 27; v, 20, *municipatus.*

39. Col. 3 : 11; *Sib. Or.* viii, 127.

CHAPTER IV

JEWISH

W hile the purpose of these chapters is to illustrate the Book of Acts from contemporary history, we need not forget that illustration in the reverse direction is possible. Just as our Gospels are themselves a source for our knowledge of Judaism in Palestine in the first century, so the Book of Acts and other Christian sources are to be welcomed by students of Judaism as additions to the limited knowledge which Jewish writers like Josephus give us.

But the Book of Acts is perhaps even more valuable for the impression it gives of Judaism not in Palestine but in the so-called Diaspora or Dispersion. Except for part of Philo I can think of no narrative preserved from the same period whose scene is laid so largely in the Jewish circles of the eastern Mediterranean outside of Palestine. Synagogues are mentioned in Damascus (plural, 9 : 2, 20), in Salamis on Cyprus (plural, 13 : 5), in Antioch of Pisidia (13 : 14), in Iconium (14 : 1), in Thessalonica (17 : 1), in Athens (17 : 17), in Corinth (18 : 4, 7), and in Ephesus (18 : 19, 26). While literary sources and particularly recent excavations indicate the extent of the synagogue, for example in Northern Galilee, at Dura-Europos on the Euphrates and in Rome, for most of the above places Acts is our only evidence. The most famous exception is the fragment of an inscription at Corinth which apparently read '[syna]gogue of the Hebr[ews]'.[1] Luke evidently took the institution for granted practically everywhere—if we may judge from the phrase used in connection with Gentile converts to Christianity: 'For Moses from early generations has had in every city those who preach him, for he is read in the synagogues on every sabbath' (Acts 15 : 21). The universality and the antiquity of the synagogue—if as seems likely, Luke here exaggerates them—are probably equally exaggerated in Jewish writers. Philo speaks of 'thousands of houses of instruction' opened on the sabbath day,[2] and the Rabbis quite fancifully carried the institution, which is of exilic origin probably, back as far at least as the time of the patriarch Jacob.[3] It is the more striking that at one place instead of synagogue the author of Acts uses another word, 'place of prayer'. This is at Philippi by the riverside (16: 13). Of course it is possible that the word is synonymous and is used by the author where he might as well have used synagogue. But it is tempting to suppose that some reason which escapes us accounts not only for his different term but also for his strange expression 'we *supposed* there was a place of prayer'.

Our author mentions without synagogue other individual and collective examples of his phrase 'all the Jews among the Gentiles' (21: 21), e.g. Jews in Phoenicia and Cyprus and at Antioch of Syria (11: 19), Timothy and his mother at Lystra or Derbe (16: 1) with other Jews in the neighbourhood (16: 3), Aquila of Pontus (18: 2) and Apollos of Alexandria (18: 24). With Aquila are mentioned the Jews expelled with him from Rome, with Apollos the Jews that he refuted in Achaia (18: 28). In the province of Asia we have not only the synagogue at Ephesus and the Jewish family of Sceva and his seven sons (19: 14) but reference to both Jews and Greeks residing in Ephesus (19: 17) and both Jews and Greeks residing in Asia (19: 10). That our author mentions at Rome the Jews (28: 17) but not any of the synagogues there of which we now know is perhaps due to the fact that Paul was not free to attend them.

Even in Jerusalem our author is aware of the presence of Diaspora Jews. We know that they took pilgrimages to the capital particularly at feasts, and so in the long list of localities represented at Pentecost the people are usually thought to be Jewish representatives. This may be wrong, and in any case the author is interested more in their languages—perhaps originally twelve—or their geographical distribution than in their religion. Jews at Jerusalem are mentioned more definitely elsewhere in Acts. Thus of the many synagogues in Jerusalem (24: 12) Acts mentions in one passage at least one synagogue, perhaps five

synagogues, belonging to one or more of the Jewish groups of
the dispersion. The list of five names is suggestive (6 : 9). First
Libertini or enfranchised slaves or freedmen, then Cyrenians and
Alexandrians, and finally those of Cilicia and Asia. The existence
at Jerusalem of a synagogue of the Alexandrians is known to us
from Jewish sources.[4] The purchase of it by a rabbi near the end
of the first century is an item creating considerable discussion as
to whether synagogues may be bought and sold.

The term *libertini* in a list of geographical terms seems out of
place. For that reason modern scholars have looked for substi-
tutes and the obvious and independently repeated conjecture is a
name like Libystini or Libyans, from a country lying between
Alexandria and Cyrene.[5] As early as the seventh century a Greek
writer either read or conjectured a reference to Libya here.[6]
But the libertini is not impossible and Luke's use of 'so called' is
his usual apology for retaining or translating non-Greek terms.
Libertinus as a Latin term had once meant a son of a freedman
or *libertus*. Before the end of the Roman republic it meant the
freedman himself and not his children.[7] We know from Tacitus
and others that there were many Jews who were freedmen in
Italy in the first century A.D.[8] Why not in Jerusalem itself, in
association with other Jews from abroad?

A synagogue of Libertini is wrongly said to have been proved
for Pompeii. For Jerusalem the nearest we have as yet for evidence of what the King James Version called a synagogue of
Libertines is an inscription from about A.D. 70 found there, first
published in 1914.[9] It tells that a certain Theodotus 'built the
synagogue for the reading of the law and for the teaching of the
commandments and the guest house and the rooms and the sup-
plies of water as an inn for those who have need when coming
from abroad'. This institution was apparently an old family
beneficiary. The inscription says that Theodotus' fathers and the
elders and Simonides had built the synagogue. Like him, his
father and grandfather had held office as ruler of the synagogue.
The hint that the family may have been freedmen is in the
father's Roman name Vettenus, a name of the sort which slaves
of Romans took when freed from slavery.

The presence of Cyrenian Jews is probably further attested by the mention by our author in his gospel (following Mark) of Simon of Cyrene at Jerusalem. For Cilician Jews at Jerusalem Paul himself is sufficient example, and perhaps his sister's son (23 : 16). Jews of the province of Asia appear in Jerusalem. It was they who recognizing a Gentile fellow countryman of theirs in company with Paul, Trophimus of Ephesus, raised the charge that Paul had taken a non-Jew into the Temple (21: 27–29). In addition to these countries mentioned among the Jewish opponents of Stephen, Jews from Cyprus appear in Barnabas (4 : 36) and Mnason, though whether the latter was a Jew and just where he was living are questions that are not quite clear (21 : 16). Evidently the author implies that among those who were scattered as far as Antioch upon the persecution that followed Stephen's death in Judaea several Cypriotes and Cyrenians were included (11 : 20), though he mentions by name only one of each at Antioch, Barnabas of Cyprus and Lucius of Cyrene (13 : 1).

Presumably in all these cases the individuals were of Jewish blood as well as Jewish faith. Barnabas a Levite and Paul of the tribe of Benjamin surely were. Acts rarely mentions proselytes, but often enough to indicate that the writer knew the distinction. It is interesting that the only proselyte whose name or home is given, Nicolas a proselyte from Antioch, comes precisely from a city at which Josephus tells us that the proselytes were especially abundant. It might be supposed that we could distinguish as of alien blood the proselytes by their Gentile names. The trouble is that pure blooded Jews often had Greek names themselves. Among early Christians of Jewish origin we may mention Andrew and Philip in the Gospels. The names of both are Greek. In Thomas called Didymus we have first the Aramaic and then the Greek word for 'twin'. In Acts an alphabetic list of Greek and Latin named Jews would begin Aeneas of Lydda, Alexander of Ephesus, Apollos of Alexandria, Aquila of Pontus, Aristarchus of Thessalonica, while in the following double names the second member is distinctly Latin: Joseph Justus, John Marcus, Saul-Paulus, Silas-Silvanus.[10] The first of these pairs curiously coincides with one of the rabbinic passages against Jews taking on foreign names in which faithful Jews are reminded that the twelve patriarchs when in Egypt did not change their names, Reuben to Rufus, Joseph to Justus, etc. When a non-Jewish name was adopted in addition to a Jewish one it often had some connection of sound or meaning with the original. Tabitha and Dorcas mean in Aramaic and Greek respectively gazelle (Acts 9 : 36). Thus the Hebrews named Benjamin often reappear in European languages named wolf,—Wolf in German or English, Loup in French, Lupo in Italian, and Lobo in Spanish. That is obviously due to the prophecy of Jacob in Genesis 49 : 27, 'Benjamin is a wolf that raveneth'. My learned colleague—who himself is called Professor Wolfson—has suggested that the same is true of Joseph Justus of Acts 1: 23, for a very common epithet of the patriarch Joseph, especially in Arabic and cabalistic Judaism, is *sadiq* 'upright'. But Jews with other names in J probably had the same distinguishing by-name, like Jesus Justus (Col. 4: 11) and James, the brother of the Lord, called the Just in early Christian writings. Probably other Jewish names lie behind other Greek and Latin names in Acts as they do behind modern non-Hebrew names of Jews.[11] We may not conclude as is too often done from the Greek names of the Seven (6 : 5) that these men were Gentiles or even Jews of the dispersion because they all bear Greek names. No doubt the practice of substitution would be more common in non-Semitic areas though at this time few areas were entirely Semitic. Persons of other cultures did the same thing as is shown *inter alia* by many inscriptions where the parent's name reveals the alien origin of persons with good Greek or Latin names. The reverse relation of names is quite unusual. An Egyptian papyrus of A.D. 194 is a request of Eudaemon son of Psois and Tiathres for permission to call himself Eudaemon son of Heron and Didyme.[12] The new Greek names of his parents have the same meaning as the old Egyptian ones. But no doubt it would hurt Eudaemon's social standing in some circles to be introduced as son of Psois and Tiathres.

Beside testifying to the presence of actual Jews in the dispersion, the author of Acts gives the impression of an abundance of partial adherents to Judaism in the communities that figure in his story. This at least is what his phrase God-fearers or God-worshippers is commonly understood to mean. His usage may however be not quite technical though Jewish writings both Greek and Aramaic have been claimed to have a similar term—in the latter fearers of heaven, with the usual Jewish substitute for the word God. Even Juvenal is thought to mention such a 'fearer'. Above all we must avoid the old error of interpreting in this sense the rabbinic 'proselytes of the gate'. That the phrase in Acts is not technical of the Gentile adherents of Judaism is suggested not only by its use of Jews themselves[13] and of proselytes (13 : 43) but by its employment of certain worshippers of the Most High God in the north shore of the Black Sea disclosed by first century inscriptions found in that remote area. Not only 'reverer' but also 'Most High God' and even προσευχή as a place of worship are used in these inscriptions and these as well as the actual 'synagogue of the Jews' are taken in a Jewish sense. It is claimed they are all due to Jewish influence. But it is quite plain that other deities are known there beside the god of the Jews, and, while it is true that Most High God is often used as it is in Acts itself (16 : 17) as the appropriate term by which a non-Jew may refer to the Jewish god, it is much more widespread in use than that, and even when employed with no explicit reference to a pagan deity does not necessarily mean 'Yahweh'.

The upshot of this long parenthesis and of the much longer and more complicated discussion in other books[14] is therefore that we cannot press the passages in Acts as indicating that in nearly a dozen cases the author is referring in a semi-technical way to a common phenomenon in antiquity, that is to partial adherents to Judaism. There can be no doubt however that the phenomenon was common, and that it must have played a large part in the first spread of Christianity in cities where the stricter Jews rejected Christ crucified as a stumbling block. Unfortunately neither Acts nor any other source can be quoted as actual evidence.

What is rather more explicitly stated in Acts is that Judaism was the centre of opposition to Christianity. Again and again the

Jews take the initiative against Paul, and plots of the Jews are a kind of refrain running through his life. In the fine phrase of Tertullian the synagogues were the 'fountains of persecution'.[15] Once more we raise the question: Can this feature of Judaism as presented in Acts be confirmed from outside sources? Beside Tertullian who is much later there is little evidence. Paul once (1 Thess. 2 : 15) definitely says that the Jews in Judea not only 'killed Jesus and the prophets, but also drove out us . . . forbidding us to speak to the Gentiles that they may be saved'. But his allusions elsewhere to the Jews as rejecting the gospel do not carry any implication that they attempted to hinder it. With this lack of confirmation the impression which Acts gives of continuous malevolent activity of the Jews everywhere against the gospel has been seriously discounted by Jewish scholars, while some Christian scholars also have been inclined to regard this feature of Acts as editorial monotone rather than historical information. Certainly the Jew in Justin Martyr's dialogue is friendly. But Justin himself has half a dozen passages in which he definitely accuses the Jews not merely of rejecting Jesus and the gospel but of persecuting as far as it was in their power those who believed in Christ. And beside later scattering evidence from the martyr literature[16] we have within the era of Acts the obscure or indirect evidence of the Book of Revelation and of the Gospels. Certainly the latter with their emphasis on Jews in controversy with Jesus and with their definite predictions for the disciples of excommunication from the synagogues or worse at the hands of the Jews would never have been written as they are without some contemporary parallels and confirmation *ex eventu*.

Whatever the relations of Jews and Christians may have been, there is increasing evidence that the Jews were themselves the objects of a good deal of popular dislike on the part of the Gentiles. A series of modern discoveries has revealed a group of stories of anti-Semitic tendency written and read by Greeks in Egypt. Usually they have to do with friction between the two parties in Alexandria and the transfer of the dispute to Rome. Like more recent anti-Semitic protocols these narratives are almost certainly forgeries, or, if the term is preferable, fiction.

The dialogue with the mutual calling of names is very sprightly. The accounts are not contemporary or at least they are read much later—'heathen martyr acts' they have been called because like the Christian *acta martyrum* they seem to have become a kind of literary effort. In them the Jews usually enjoy the Emperor's favour and the Gentiles are given short shrift.[17]

The interest of these pieces for the student of Acts is that the scene is laid in the very century of the latter and in the cities of Alexandria and Rome where conditions must have been not unlike those in the places more conspicuous in Acts. We are not without more contemporary and trustworthy evidence. Philo at some length describes what today would be called pogroms. In his own time they occurred in Alexandria. In fact he himself was a member of a Jewish delegation to Rome to deal with the issue. Josephus writing a little later also treats of conditions between Jew and Gentile in Alexandria. He has the further advantage for us that he records the problems of Jewish status in other Greek cities. Finally there has recently been found the text of an official letter of the Emperor Claudius addressed partly to the Jewish and partly to the Greek population of Alexandria and dealing with the friction between them.

Now there was no partisan reason why such Jewish-Gentile tension should find any expression in the Book of Acts. For the author both groups stand in contrast to Christianity. There are, however, several passages where such friction may be evidenced, though never as clearly as we should like. When for example at Philippi the charge is made against Paul and Silas: 'These men are disturbing our city and they are Jews and they are announcing customs which it is illegal for us to accept or to do, seeing we are Romans,' we may well ask the question, is the accuser appealing to the magistrates' duty as Romans to see that a Roman colony is not harbouring a forbidden religious custom,[18] or is he appealing to their general anti-Jewish prejudice to suppress these visiting Jewish teachers? Again at Corinth when the Jews failed to get Gallio to condemn Paul but rather were driven by him away from the Bench, we read, 'and they all took Sosthenes, the ruler of the synagogue and beat him before the

Bench. And Gallio was not troubled at all by these things.' Who are 'they all'? Is the author here suggesting that when the Jews were unsuccessful the Gentiles in Corinth turned the tables on them by violence against their leader? At least some early scribes thought so and wrote: 'And all the Greeks,' etc. So also at Ephesus a demonstration in the theatre intended against Christianity appears really to turn against the Jews: 'At the instigation of the Jews some of the crowd put forward Alexander, and Alexander motioned with his hand and wished to make a defence to the people. But when they recognized that he was a Jew there was a single cry from them all, howling for about two hours, "Great is Artemis of the Ephesians! great is Artemis of the Ephesians!" ' Certainly these passages look like specimens of mob Jew-baiting as it took place in the cities of the ancient world. Does our author so understand them? And does he tell them with a little malicious glee—noting that the arch enemies of the Christians when trying to work against the gospel were themselves the victims of mob malice, while the authorities either winked sympathetically at the performance, as Gallio did, or like the Asiarchs at Ephesus saw to it that Paul was not exposed to the mob? There are scholars who think the severe words of Claudius in his letter to the Alexandrian Jewry were likewise a boomerang result of their controversy with the Christians and the same explanation precisely is sometimes given to the obscure words of Suetonius: *Judaeos assidue tumultuantes Chresto impulsore*, in reference to Claudius' expulsion of Jews from Rome.[19] It will be recalled that this expulsion was by an imperial decree which our author also mentions in explaining the recent arrival at Corinth from Italy of Aquila and Priscilla (18 : 2).

Punishment of Jews comes from another quarter in the case of Sceva's seven sons. As exorcists or magicians they used illegitimately the magic power of the name of Jesus whom Paul preached, until one of the possessed turned upon them, and they fled from the place naked and wounded (19 : 13-16).

One feature of Judaism's part in the dispersion that until recently would have seemed peculiar is illustrated in Acts in the story of Sceva's sons just referred to and in that of the 'Jewish false prophet', Elymas, at Cyprus (13 : 6), namely the prominence of Jewish influence in contemporary magic. Of course magic was in that cosmopolitan age one of the most syncretistic of arts—and many sources or cultures were laid under contribution, including Egyptian and Chaldaean as the most venerated of them. But the Jews too with their old and barbarian literature, with their imageless worship and their claim to know the unpronounceable name of the creator of the world, with their native practice of exorcism and even, in spite of Mosaic prohibitions, of sheer magic, easily acquired prestige in the dispersion though doubtless to the loss of prestige among their orthodox brethren. We recall that Jesus in the Talmud is regarded as a magician. In the story of Sceva's sons they are spoken of as only some of the Jewish itinerant exorcists in Ephesus, while their father is actually called a Jewish chief priest. The modern discoveries on papyrus of the actual books of ancient Greek magic show the influence not only of intelligently used Old Testament passages but the mixing in, as of mystifying hocus pocus, of many untranslated Semitic words. One recalls how when that archcharlatan Alexander of Abonuteichos professed to be a prophet introducing a new cult of two Greek gods 'he uttered certain unintelligible sounds like those of Hebrews or Phoenicians and impressed the audience, since it did not know what he said except that he mixed Apollo and Asclepius in among them.'[20] Doubtless we are to suppose that in some such way the sons of Sceva brought in the names of Jesus and Paul.

As for the parts of the story of Acts that are placed in Palestine it is possible to get some confirmation from Palestinian archaeology, while for illustration from the religion of Palestinian Jewry in Talmud and Midrash we depend on Billerbeck's excellent commentary.[21] The places named in Jerusalem are often too vaguely indicated for any identification to be possible—like the Field of Blood, the upper room mentioned after the ascension, the house of Mary the mother of John Mark, the place of Stephen's stoning—though of course Christian local tradition cherishes one or more sites for each with credulous piety. Different groups of Christians in modern Jerusalem claim four different places for the last moments of the proto-martyr, Stephen, but we cannot be quite sure today even where the city wall ran at the time, the wall outside of which the execution of Stephen and probably of Jesus also took place. Public buildings like the Beautiful Gate, Solomon's Porch, the Roman praetorium have more chance of exact identification. At least their general location can be indicated, but only of the last are actual remains at all likely. Recent excavations have shown in a proper section of the city an old paving which might even be the Gabbatha where Jesus was brought before Pilate, and the site of Paul's conversation with later Roman authorities.[22] Perhaps the most satisfactory single archaeological object connected with this part of Acts is the inscribed block of stone now in the museum in Istanbul discovered in 1871 by Clermont-Ganneau containing one of the Greek inscriptions which warned Gentiles not to pass the balustrade into the inner court of the Temple. It was so satisfactory that skilful natives promptly forged several duplicates.[23] It was past this balustrade that Paul was accused of introducing Gentiles like Trophimus (21 : 28, 29).

In a less direct way the recently discovered evidence of Jewish sects previously unknown throws light on the setting of the Book of Acts. For Christianity as there portrayed is a new 'sect' or 'fellowship' (24 : 25; 2 : 42) within the bosom of the Jewish community. Like the other sects Christianity did not, at least at first, reject anything that was central in Judaism, its God, or Law or Temple. It developed new emphases or new strictness and a new understanding of the scriptures. It would be premature to draw too many inferences from the scrolls from the Dead Sea area of which only a few have been published so far, or even from the kindred fragments of Zadokite or Damascus covenanters literature, though these have been known for a few decades. They do indicate in general the initial hospitality of Judaism to the continuing arising of sects, with new interpretations of the past prophets, and the expectation of a new one. There is even coincidence with Acts in the Old Testament passages they quote, and in the curse of severe punishment due to those who lie about their private property. The newly found documents contemplate as does Acts a sharing of such property. Since they are in Semitic rather than Greek the degree of equivalence between their vocabulary and that of Acts is not easily determined.[24] They are, however, likely to prove an extensive help to our placing of the Book of Acts in Jewish history.

The external evidence to Jewish history in some cases deals with identifiable individuals in Acts. While the Gospels speak generally of false Messiahs as likely to come, the author of Acts mentions at least three such leaders of secession and revolt, and all these appear also in Josephus,—Theudas, Judas of Galilee and the Egyptian false leader. Dates and numbers do not always fit but probably the same persons are meant by the Christian as by the Jewish historian. The contemporary Jewish rulers mentioned in Acts also fit into our other sources of knowledge. In the earlier generation we have Herod (Agrippa) who executed James and arrested Peter. The account of his death in Acts 12 forms an interesting basis for comparison with Josephus[25] in dealing with the same event. In the next generation we have his daughters Bernice and Drusilla and his son (Herod) Agrippa. The four high priests named in Acts 4: 6 are an embarrassment of riches since no John or Alexander is known. Gamaliel, the only rabbi or scribe to be mentioned by name in the New Testament is mentioned in Acts twice (5: 34; 22: 3) and also in the Jewish sources.

One of the links with environment which we have already mentioned several times is the occurrence of appropriate personal names. I will not repeat here all that I have written elsewhere about characteristic Jewish names in Acts.[26] There are many of them, some of them repeated several times over: Judas (six of them), Simon and John (four of each), James and Ananias (three of each). Beside these commoner names the Semitic patronymic Bar is obvious not only in Barnabas, which if it comes from Nebo can be scarcely called originally Jewish, but also in Bar-Jesus, Bartholomew (13: 8; 1: 13) and in Barsabbas. This last name 'strangely enough occurs of not one but two figures in Acts not otherwise connected. One, like Barnabas, has the name Joseph (1: 23), the other is Judas Barsabbas (15: 22).

Both are Jews of Jerusalem, and there can be little doubt that the name is of Semitic and specifically of Aramaic origin. The best Greek evidence is for the double *beta* spelling ($Bαρσαββᾶς$) a form naturally connected with the word Sabbath'.[27] Greek names similar, but without the bar—Sabas, Sambas, Sabbaios, Sabbion, Sabbataeus, Sabbatis, Sambathaeus—occur not only in Palestine but of Jews in Egypt and Rome. It is very likely that the name was given originally to children born on the sabbath.

Another and rarer name is that of Sapphira, wife and accomplice of the famous liar Ananias. It might be regarded as a Greek name but no such woman's name is known to us from Greek sources nor are any Jewish parallels cited in the dictionaries. Not long ago, however, Professor Sukenik of Jerusalem collected the names scratched upon ossuaries, which were the form of burial urns employed in Jerusalem and its environs in the centuries just before and after the time of Christ. He has noted at least four different persons whose names are given as Sapphira both in Aramaic (two spellings) and in Greek (three spellings). 'Thus for the first time we have conclusive evidence outside the New Testament and from Jerusalem itself of the currency in both Aramaic and Greek of a woman's name Sapphira.'[28]

In Luke's relation to current Judaism it is possible to go somewhat deeper than the physical and tangible phenomena that we have mentioned and to show his accordance in some areas with Jewish thought. I refer particularly to his treatment of Old Testament history in his speeches. I am not now raising the question whether these speeches are in any real sense derived from actual speeches delivered by the original actors. Whether they are or are not, in so far as they can be confirmed by contemporary Jewish sources, they offer us examples of the relation of the book to its environment—in short of its place in history.

Just as the speech at Athens quoted from 'some' of the poets[29] so several of the more Jewish scenes in the book echo and actually quote the Jewish scriptures of the Old Testament. Such

use of a written book would still not carry us very far into a
conviction of Luke's accord with Judaism. The Bible he quotes
is the Greek translation not the original Hebrew, and that of
course was accessible to Greek-speaking Gentiles. It was also the
Bible employed by nearly every early Christian of whom we
know. There is nothing peculiarly Jewish then in Luke's ability
in his addresses in Acts to reproduce the story or to quote the
words which we can still read in our Septuagint.

When, however, as not infrequently is the case, the speeches
differ from the contents of the Old Testament or add features
not there recorded, we may inquire whether these traits are
simply errors, or personal interpretations of Luke or his speakers,
or whether they have some confirmation in non-canonical
Jewish writings or in the oral tradition which other writers elsewhere record. The evidence of this latter sort is certainly interesting and it is fairly abundant.

One recalls for example the statement made in the first great
speech in Acts, that at Pentecost, to the effect that David the
Patriarch 'both died and was buried and his tomb is with us
unto this day'. The method of argument is characteristically
Jewish. The book of Psalms is being quoted. Although it is
known to consist of different poems, it is treated as all by David,
much as our same author quotes the Book of the Twelve as 'the
prophets' without differentiating the authors. Now the pronoun of the first person in the Psalms might be thought to belong to David. But according to the rabbis' method of interpretation scripture had another pervasive personality,—the Messiah. If a scripture writer is not referring to himself he may be
speaking of the Messiah. So when the Ethiopian asks of the Fifty
Third Chapter of Isaiah, 'Of whom speaketh the prophet this?
of himself or of some other?' Philip 'beginning from this scripture preached unto him Jesus'. So Peter at Pentecost wishing to
prove that the promise of resurrection in Psalm 16: 'Thou wilt
not leave my soul in Hades neither wilt thou suffer thy Holy one
to see corruption' refers not to David but to that other, reminds
his hearers, as it is put elsewhere, 'David in his own generation
having served the will of God, fell asleep (i.e. died) and was

added to his fathers (i.e. was buried) and saw corruption'
(13 : 36).[30]

To add to the proof the Book of Acts makes a contemporary
reference about David's burial: 'His tomb is with us to this
day.' It is the kind of argument used by Greek philosophers and
atheists about the tomb of Zeus. As in the very different context,
perhaps alluded to elsewhere in Acts (17: 28),[31] the tomb of
Zeus which is pointed out to sightseers in Crete is good evidence
that Zeus is no god, so the tomb of David in first century Jerusalem is good evidence that it cannot be said of David that he
did not see corruption. Now of course the Book of Kings tells
us of David, as it does indeed systematically of each of his royal
descendants generally, that he 'slept with his fathers and was
buried in the city of David'. An observant Jewish critic of the
later time says there were no graves in Jerusalem except of
David and his family and of the prophetess Huldah.[32] But no
real evidence of the existence in later days of anything purport-
ing to be royal tombs at Jerusalem is forthcoming in biblical or
rabbinic writings. We have however complete confirmation
from other sources and exactly for the Herodian period of
Jewish history in two passages in Josephus[33] and in an inscription. The inscription is not for David but for a later king,
Uzziah, and though found in Jerusalem many years ago has only
lately been deciphered. It reads in an Aramaic script of the era:

> Hither were brought the bones of Uzziah.
> Do not open.[34]

Nicolas of Damascus, a historian contemporary with Herod
the Great, though his work is now lost, evidently referred to an
expensive construction of white marble with which that
monarch decorated the tomb of David, while Josephus refers to
a theft of three thousand talents of silver from one room of the
tomb by John Hyrcanus and to a later attempt by Herod the
Great to secure further spoils.

Has the Pentecost story any features which might echo
Jewish tradition about that feast? For it should be recalled that
Pentecost was a Jewish feast, the Old Testament Feast of Weeks,

and is mentioned as such in giving the date in Acts. This is a fact that Christians who think of it primarily in connection with the story in Acts need to remember. Probably when the author of Acts wrote neither Pentecost nor even the first day of the week (20: 7) were as yet Christian dates. Indeed one of the Jewish features of Acts is precisely this use of Jewish dating. This is perhaps natural for even a non-Jew when the story he tells has to do with Jerusalem and with individuals or crowds attending feasts there. Thus we have not only the reference to the first Pentecost of the story of Acts, and to the Passover after which Herod Agrippa intended to kill Peter, but also to a later Pentecost and, according to the Western Text, another feast (18: 21) which Paul hoped to attend. What is more striking is that what seem to us mere data about sailing are described more than once with reference to Jewish feasts quite away from Jerusalem. At 20: 6 we read 'but we sailed after the days of un-leavened bread from Philippi' and in 27: 9 (another 'we' passage) the author observed that 'a long time had passed' in getting from Myra to Fair Havens 'and the voyage was already dangerous because even the Fast was already over'. *The* Fast was certainly the Jewish day of Atonement (Yom Kippur). There is evidence that the later Rabbis referred to the adjacent date in the Jewish calendar, the Feast of Tabernacles, as marking the end of safe navigation. It is possible that Paul and such Jews as were with him had actually celebrated the day. If there were Jews on Crete they too would have done so. We know from both Josephus and Philo that Jews on Crete were numerous. We know from inscriptions that a century or more earlier the Jews on the island of Delos usually observed the day. But we cannot infer that this is why the author mentions the day in this very Gentile context, any more than we can infer that the Ascension of Jesus occurred on a Saturday from the fact that this same author describes the place of the Ascension from which the disciples returned to the city as a Sabbath day's journey from Jerusalem. These Jewish measures for distance and time are both strange, when good Gentile terms were available for both, e.g stadia (a term which our author himself does use (Luke 24: 13) in measuring the distance of another village, Emmaus, from Jerusalem) and the Gentile names for months or seasons.

But to return to what Christians somewhat erroneously call the first Pentecost—shall we suppose that in mentioning the tomb of David, Peter or his biographer is here aware of the tradition which appears later among the rabbis that David died on a feast of Pentecost? And shall we suppose that in describing the distribution of tongues and the miraculous comprehension of the gospel preaching the author is aware of any tradition that God gave the law to Moses on the day of Pentecost and that the voice of the Almighty at that time divided into seventy voices, so that every nation might hear the divine commandments in its own language?

Questions of this sort can be asked with more hope of certain answers if we turn to that larger assembly of Old Testament references—the longest speech in Acts.[35] Although it is reported as delivered as a defence from Jewish charges against Stephen it is in fact Stephen's charges against the Jews. At first sight it seems to begin merely as a review of Jewish history, but definite motives of a polemic character run through it from the start. I am not now so much concerned with these motives as I am with the discrepancies between the Old Testament story and the summary in Acts. Let me list some of them:

In the Old Testament God appeared to Abraham at Haran and told him to migrate. In Acts he appeared to Abraham before his earlier migration from Ur of the Chaldees to Haran.

In the Old Testament the account of Abraham's leaving Haran is told after his father's death, and so Acts definitely dates his departure. But the chronology of Genesis if examined dates it before his father's death.

In the Old Testament Jacob's family is reckoned as seventy persons, in Acts as seventy-five.

In the Old Testament Abraham buys a burial place from Ephron at Machpelah and Jacob buys a piece of ground near Shechem from the sons of Hamor, while in Acts Abraham buys a tomb at Shechem from the sons of Emmor (Hamor) or buys a tomb from Shechem the father of Hamor.

In the Old Testament Jacob is buried at Hebron, Joseph at Shechem. In Acts both they and all the patriarchs are buried at the same place, namely Shechem.

As it is with the life of the patriarchs so with the life of Moses. The following traits in the account of Acts are not in the Old Testament at all. As an infant he was beautiful before God; he was educated in the wisdom of the Egyptians; he was forty years old when he fled to Midian and it was forty years later when he returned; the sea in which Pharaoh was overthrown was the Red Sea; and the law was delivered to Moses by an angel.

Now where did Acts get these different ideas or to what are they due? Some of them are doubtless cases of mere confusion. The parallel accounts merged in Genesis make it easy to confuse dates, events, etc., that are similar, and often the Old Testament itself has a very confused view or two contradictory ones. Many of these variations in Acts are just like the slips that an inaccurate theological student might make today in trying to retell the patriarchal history. In other cases Acts is merely following the Septuagint version, as indeed it does elsewhere, to the extent of fully half the words in the speech and some of the items that we have noted, like seventy-five in Jacob's family [36] or the name 'Red Sea'. But the striking thing about so many of the other changes is that they are nearly all attested in other Jewish writings.

The vision of God to Abraham in Ur is mentioned in both Philo and Josephus, while Philo also states that Terah was dead when Abraham left Haran. Similarly about Moses, Philo and Josephus agree with Acts in describing him as a baby of divinely beautiful form, while Philo emphasizes his Egyptian education. The sentence on Moses 'doing wonders and signs in Egypt and at the Red Sea and in the desert forty years' has an exact and extensive verbal parallel in the apocryphal work, *The Assumption of Moses*: 'who suffered many things in Egypt and in the Red Sea and in the desert forty years'. For the angel at the giving of the law—twice mentioned in Stephen's speech, we have not only the agreement of Josephus and Philo but the writers of the two Christian epistles, Galatians and Hebrews, and of the two apocryphal writings, the *Testaments of the Twelve Patriarchs* and the *Book of Jubilees*.

While some of these and some other traits in the speech have parallels in the rabbis—that is, in Palestinian and Aramaic tradition, it is evident that Luke could have secured many of them from Hellenistic or Greek speaking Judaism. The coincidences with Philo and Josephus are too numerous to be accidental and we must therefore posit somewhere either in Luke himself or in the material that he is using not merely a direct knowledge of the Old Testament in its Greek translation but an acquaintance with certain embellishments or interpretations of its story that had circulation in Jewish and Jewish Christian circles. In so doing we are discovering another contact of our author with the less external phenomena of contemporary Judaism.

There are other variations of the speech from the Hebrew Old Testament. For example the passage from Amos in Acts 7: 42 f. differs in important ways from the Hebrew as does another quotation from Amos in Acts 15: 16-18. But these changes had occurred in the Septuagint from which the author regularly quotes—a fact which makes improbable the theory of direct dependence of this part of Acts on a Christian Aramaic original. It may be worth noting that precisely the same two passages of Amos are quoted in a single passage in the Hebrew uncanonical Zadokite document (9: 4-9), and that Justin Martyr brings together just as Acts does (7: 42 f., 49 f.) the passage from Amos 5 and that from Isaiah 66.[37] A tradition of association of passages is as good evidence of Jewish background for Acts as changes of fact or wording.

Some of the variants of Acts from the Old Testament I have not been able to parallel from Jewish sources. Thus the replacement of 'beyond Damascus' by 'beyond Babylon' may be original with this author,—intentional but natural, though 'to Babylon' would be still more natural. But there is one item in this list of variants from the Old Testament which seems to me to carry us a little deeper into the author's own reaction to Jewish prejudice. I have already noted the confusion of Shechem where Joseph was buried and Hebron where Jacob was buried.

It was natural to combine the two and to add reference to the burial of Jacob's other sons, Joseph's brothers. The latter is related not only here but by Josephus and the *Book of Jubilees* and seems to underlie also the *Testaments of the Twelve Patriarchs*. But the place is not Shechem as in Acts but Hebron. While either site would have been a natural simplification of the Old Testament story I am convinced that in Acts an *arrière-pensée* lies behind that word Shechem.

An important animus in the whole speech is an attack upon the alleged privileges of the Jews. They claimed—to use Paul's terms—the inheritance, the giving of the Law, the shekinah; but Stephen's speech urges that the Law has been broken, that the Temple with its sacrificial worship was not divinely intended, and that the land of Canaan in the patriarchs' day was not really owned by them. In one place Stephen says God gave to Abraham as immediate possession not so much as a pace's length of land—but later he refers to a place which Abraham did own having bought and paid for it—a burial place where the great patriarchs had their tombs. It was the burial place at Shechem.

Now when one recalls that Shechem was the sacred city of the Samaritans the polemic bias of Stephen's allusion to it here is evident. To claim that the only real inheritance of the fathers to which the Jews had a long established title was precisely the headquarters of hated heresy is the most biting form of anti-Jewish polemic. In Jewish literature of an orthodox type we have many evidences of subtle slurs, omissions, emendations and the like all intended to put the Samaritan city in its right perspective.[38] The author of Chronicles-Ezra-Nehemiah in rewriting the Book of Kings had omitted entirely the history of the Northern or Samaritan Kingdom. Josephus also, paraphrasing in his *Antiquities* the biblical record, makes changes in historical detail motivated by the later Jewish prejudice against Samaria. Another re-writing of history, the *Biblical Antiquities* of Pseudo-Philo, deals with the period from Genesis through Samuel. A study of this document discloses its varied and interesting anti-Samaritan technique. It abbreviates or re-locates the episodes which the Bible had placed in Shechem and other northern localities, or it reports them in speeches rather than in narrative, and thus escapes the necessity of any geographical location.[39] But our author in Acts with a characteristic critique of Jewish self-satisfaction has lugged in the claim to honour of the despised Shechem. Just as in two narratives in the same writer's Gospel a Samaritan appears to great advantage to the shaming of the Jew,[40] so here our author seems again deliberately to be flouting Jewish prejudice against the Samaritan. And one may recall further how in the same Gospel another address, which like Stephen's speech ends with attempted lynching of the speaker, features the facts so unpalatable to Jewish patriotism: 'There were many widows in Israel in the days of Elijah when . . . there came a great famine over all the land and unto none of them was Elijah sent but only to Zarephath in the land of Sidon. And there were many lepers in Israel in the time of Elisha the prophet, and none of them was cleansed but only Naaman the Syrian.'[41] It is the same spirit that breathes in the passage before us, which we might paraphrase: There are many patriotic shrines of orthodox Judaism in the land of Israel today, but not one of them has claim to continuous Hebrew ownership or early divine gift to the patriarchs except the Samaritan city of Shechem.

In such subtle references to Jewish prejudice perhaps more clearly than in his more explicit use of external local colour is to be found convincing evidence of our author's knowledge of the Jewish environment of early Christianity. But he himself and his heroes are reacting against it,—and are doing so from a Christian standpoint. Stephen's speech is written with an eye on the parallelism between ancient history and the Jewish-Christian conflict. This passage therefore may provide a good transition to our next subject: the Book of Acts in Christian history.

NOTES TO CHAPTER IV

1. Even this inscription is probably two centuries later than Acts.
2. Philo, *Sp. Leg.* ii, 62 (Mangey ii, 282; Colson in Loeb Library, VII. p. 347): 'So each seventh day there stand wide open in every city (κατὰ πᾶσαν πόλιν) thousands of schools.'

3. H. L. Strack and Paul Billerbeck, *Kommentar zum Neuen Testament aus Talmud und Midrasch*, ii, 1924, p. 740.

4. Tosefta, Megillah iii, 6, 224.

5. See *Beginnings of Christianity*, iii *ad loc.*, iv *ad loc.*

6. Sophronius, who was made patriarch of Jerusalem in A.D. 633, *Anacreontea* xii, 29-30: Φαρίης (Alexandria) τε καὶ Λιβύσσης, ᾿Ασίης τε καὶ Κιλίσσης. See T. Nissen, *Philologus*, 95, 1942-3, pp. 310-313.

7. A. M. Duff, *Freedmen in the Early Roman Empire*, 1928, pp. 50-52.

8. Cf. Philo, *Leg. ad Gaium*, 23, §155.

9. R. Weill, *Comptes rendus de l'Académie des Inscriptions et Belles-Lettres*, May 29, 1914.

10. Silvanus is one of the Latin names affected by freedmen to conceal for themselves or their sons servile origin. So is Fortunatus, a name of a Corinthian Christian (1 Cor. 16: 17). See Duff, *op. cit.*, 56-58. H. Lemonnier, *Étude historique sur la condition privée des Affranchis*, 1887, deals with the names of freedmen, pp. 167-181, 304-318.

11. The habit of alternate names means also that some of the persons in Acts may be identical with persons bearing different names in Paul's letters. In the case of Silas-Silvanus this is obvious. But is Lydia of Philippi merely a Lydian woman as Ramsay thought (*Pictures of the Apostolic Church*, 1910, p. 186 and *The Bearing of Recent Discovery*, 1915, p. 309) and hence identical with one of the women in Phil. 4 : 2, Euodia or Syntyche? Goodspeed's suggestion that the Titius Justus of Acts 18 : 7 in whose house the Corinthian Christians met is the same as Gaius the host of Paul and the whole church in Corinth of Rom. 16 : 23 and that his full Roman name was Gaius Titius Justus (*Journal of Biblical Literature* 69, 1950, pp. 382-3) was also anticipated by Ramsay, *Pictures*, p. 205. Neither in Acts nor in the epistles do many companions of Paul bear Jewish names even if Jews.

12. U. Wilcken, *Grundzüge und Chrestomathie der Papyruskunde* I, ii, 1912, No. 52. In Egypt the use of names was controlled by the Roman authorities as probably by other authorities earlier. See R. Taubenschlag, *The Law of Greco-Roman Egypt in the Light of Papyri*, ii, Warsaw, 1948, pp. 50-52. See above, p. 71, on the prohibition of non-citizens taking Roman names as if citizens.

13. Acts 13 : 26 (?) and Josephus, Antiq. xiv, 7, 2.

14. *Beginnings*, v, note 8. To the earlier literature may be added the summary in M. P. Nilsson, *Geschichte der griechische Religion*, II, 1950, 636-638. See also Louis H. Feldman, 'Jewish "Sympathizers" in Classical Literature and Inscriptions,' *Transactions of the American Philological Association*, 81, 1950, pp. 200-208, and Ralph Marcus, 'The *Sebomenoi* in Josephus,' *Jewish Social Studies*, 14, 1952, pp. 247-250.

15. *Scorp.* 10: *synagogas Iudaeorum, fontes persecutionum.*

16. For example *Martyrium Polycarpi*, 12, 2; 13, 1; 17, 2. See T. Zahn *ad loc.* and A. Harnack on Papias, Fragment 11 in their edition of *Patrum Apostolicorum Opera*. A. Fridrichsen, Propter invidiam, *Eranos*, 44, 1946, pp. 161-174, believes that the ζῆλος recounted behind Christian persecutions by Clement of Rome, Epist. I, 5-6, is Jewish hostility.

17. For these Acta Alexandrinorum see H. I. Bell, *Egypt from Alexander the*

H

Great to the Arab Conquest, 1948, pp. 89 f., and note. The number of texts continues to grow. For a list of them with bibliography up to 1951 see Roger A. Pack, *op. cit.*, nos. 1732-1744 including 1736a, 1740a, 1743a in the supplement Cf. now H. A. Musurillo, *The Acts of the Pagan Martyrs, Acta Alexandrinorum*, 1954.

18. Cf. above, p. 80 (in Chapter III).

19. Cf. below, pp. 116 f, for Claudius' letter, pp. 115 f. for Chresto.

20. Lucian, *Alexander* 13.

21. See note 3.

22. Apparently it had also a Greek name 'the Pavement'. See above, p. 66, and L. H. Vincent, 'L'Antonia et le Prétoire,' *Revue Biblique*, 42, 1933, 83-113. For this and other localities in Jerusalem see *Beginnings*, v, note 35.

23. On the inscription see *Beginnings of Christianity*, iv on Acts 21 : 28. It was published by the discoverer, *Une Stèle du Temple de Jérusalem*, Paris, 1872. Two forgeries were on display in Jerusalem before the Second World War and were published by W. R. Taylor in the *Journal of the Palestine Oriental Society*, 13, 1933, 137-139; 16, 1936, 37-38. Later, in 1935, was found, too deep underground to be a modern forgery, a fragment of another original inscription, published by J. H. Iliffe, *Quarterly of the Department of Antiquities in Palestine*, 6, 1938, pp. 1-3.

24. For some of these points of comparison see what is at present the most convenient English translation of one of the documents: *The Dead Sea Manual of Discipline: Translation and Notes* by W. H. Brownlee (Bulletin of the American Schools of Oriental Research, Supplementary Studies, nos. 10-12), 1951.

25. *Antiq.* xix, 8.2§, 343-351.

26. In *Amicitiae Corolla*, ed. by H. G. Wood, 1933.

27. *Loc. cit.*, p. 48.

28. *Loc. cit.*, p. 55.

29. See above pp. 46 f.

30. The passage in Acts 2 : 33-35 continues with further evidence that a psalm does not refer to David but to Jesus. Psalm 110: 'sit thou at my right hand' was fulfilled at Jesus' ascension. 'But David did not ascend into the heavens.' J. W. Doeve, *Jewish Hermeneutics in the Synoptic Gospels and Acts*, 1953, chapter vi, finds even more elaborate midrashic techniques in these passages.

31. See above, pp. 46-49.

32. Abot of Rabbi Nathan, 35.

33. *Antiq.* xiii, 8.4; *B.J.* i, 2.5.

34. W. F. Albright, in *Bulletin of the American Schools of Oriental Research*, No. 44, December 1931, pp. 8-10.

35. For the parallels from Jewish sources to Acts 2 and 7, see notes in *Beginnings of Christianity*, iv *ad loc.*; cf. v, 114-116, 424, note 1. On Acts 7 see further Sven Carlson, *Aggadastoff i Nya Testamentets Skrifter*, Lund, 1920, pp. 101-110.

36. I understand that an unpublished Hebrew fragment found about 1953 near the Dead Sea reads at Exodus 1 : 5 seventy five like the LXX and Acts.

37. *Dial.* 22. If the association of Old Testament passages was one of the earliest forms of Christian literary effort antedating the New Testament, there

is no reason why the habit should not have been Jewish too, pre-Christian and non-Christian. Cf. Rendel Harris, *Testimonies* I, 1916, *Testimonies* II, 1920, and B. P. W. Stather Hunt, *Primitive Gospel Sources*, 1951.

38. Probably Bethuliah is substituted for Shechem to obscure the identity of the scene of the story of Judith. See C. C. Torrey, *Journal of the American Oriental Society*, 20, 1899, pp. 160–172. This is less likely the case with Sychar (John 4 : 5).

39. Abram Spiro, 'Samaritans, Tobiads, and Judahites in Pseudo-Philo,' *Proceedings of the American Academy for Jewish Research*, 20, 1951, pp. 279-355. Cf. the similar study of 'Pseudo-Philo's Saul', *ibid.*, 21, 1952, pp. 119-137. Acts 13 : 21 shows no animosity against this Benjamite king. For some indications of the anti-Samaritan treatment of history by Josephus see Spiro, *op. cit.*, 20, pp. 323-328, 337 f., 355. Spiro, *op. cit.*, 20, p. 328, note 101, promises a study of 'the familiarity of Acts with Samaritans and their traditions.' I believe Acts is more anti-Jewish and pro-Christian than pro-Samaritan.

40. Luke 10 : 33; 17 : 16.

41. Luke 4 : 25-27.

CHAPTER V

CHRISTIAN

O f all the areas of environment out of which the Book of Acts comes the innermost circle is undoubtedly the Christian. More than any other early Christian writing it is in touch with secular history and scenery, yet nevertheless it, like the others, grows out of a Christian setting. To illustrate and test this picture by the other sources of our knowledge for contemporary Christianity and to indicate something of its own contact with Christian history and its place in the varieties of Christian thought of its own time is the task of the present chapter.

If we turn to non-Christian sources for references to early Christianity we shall be largely disappointed, and those records with which our previous lectures have been concerned—Greek and Roman historians, Josephus and the rabbis, inscriptions and papyri and archaeological remains give us for the apostolic age in its Christian aspects the least possible assistance. Paul is not mentioned by a non-Christian for centuries, though pious Christian imagination as early as the fourth century fed itself on a series of forged letters between Paul and his famous contemporary, the Roman philosopher and statesman under Nero, Seneca. Of 'James the brother of Jesus the so-called Christ' the illegal execution is recorded by Josephus, perhaps that author's only reference to Christianity. The event belongs, in date, probably just after the close of Acts. So does the persecution of Christians under Nero in Rome, which is mentioned half a century afterwards in such second century writers as Tacitus and Suetonius. About the same time as these writers Pliny gives us a vivid picture of Christianity in his own day in the province of Bithynia, while later are references to Christians by Marcus Aurelius the philosopher Emperor, by Lucian the satirist and by

Galen the physician.[1] When these and the rabbinic writings refer
to the life and death of Jesus their evidence is hardly independent
of Christian tradition as prevailing in their own time. And in
any case the life and death of Jesus precede the Book of Acts and
so fall outside its scope. The non-Christian historians give no
evidence whatever about Christianity exactly contemporary
with the Book of Acts.

Our earliest archaeological evidence for Christianity is probably in the catacombs of Rome. They are extremely difficult
to date and items have often been dated much too early or
claimed as Christian with too little evidence. The phrase 'in
Christ' is doubtless decisive. It goes back in burial inscriptions
perhaps as early as the time of Hadrian. Should the ruins of
ancient Pompeii disclose any Christian reference, that would
carry us back almost if not quite to the time of Acts, i.e., to a
date before the eruption of Vesuvius, 24th of August in the year
A.D. 79. But none of the evidence thus far claimed from that site
is specifically Christian. A lamp with the monogram XP, which
was later used on the Christian labarum as containing the first
letters of 'Christ', is merely a further evidence of pre-Christian
use of that monogram. An inscription once said to contain the
word Christian was certainly misread. More romantic and pro-
phetic are the words among the *graffiti* 'Sodoma Gomorra'.
They of course could have been scratched by a Jew. One
wonders if he did it when the ashes from Vesuvius had already
begun to fall.

More recently evidence of Christianity has been sought in a
curious Latin acrostic or riddle inscribed on a pillar of the
palaestra near the amphitheatre at Pompeii, and in a cross
incised in the wall of a first floor chamber in the ruins of
Herculaneum.[2] But we have no evidence that the cross
was employed as a Christian symbol so early. The acrostic is still unexplained. It is a palindrome and it consists of
twenty-five letters arranged in a square in such a way that
beginning from any of the four sides it gives the same five
words.

```
S   A   T   O   R
A   R   E   P   O
T   E   N   E   T
O   P   E   R   A
R   O   T   A   S
```

There is nothing Christian about these five words. But it has been pointed out that the letters used are only those found in the first words of the Lord's prayer in Latin, *Pater noster*. The letters occur twice each, except N once, A and O each twice extra. The latter can be explained as Alpha and Omega (Revelation 1 : 8 *et al*), the N as the middle letter of a cross-shaped new acrostic. But again we may pertinently ask, were the Latin words *Pater noster*, familiar as they later became, really already before A.D. 79 likely to be used in this way? Or were the Latin letters A and O already widely symbolic? Even though the same formula was used probably by Roman soldiers in later times at places as remote from Italy as Cirencester in Gloucestershire and Dura-Europos on the Euphrates (the latter as early as the first half of the third century) one hesitates to make the assumption of Latin Christian liturgical influence in Pompeii four half centuries earlier.[3]

From Egypt we have today the fullest and most continuous and most intimate knowledge of the ancient world. Tens of thousands of papyri have been published representing a continuous reflection of life for a thousand years along the Nile. But Christianity appears among them first quite late.[4]

Of official documents, the first to testify to Christianity in Egypt are *libelli* from the time of Decius. These are the certificates of those who have conformed to the requirement passed by the Emperor in A.D. 249 for the purpose of stamping out Christianity. They have an almost uniform wording like the following:

To the commission of the village of Theadelphia superintending the sacrifices. From Aurelia Belle, daughter of Peteres, and her daughter Kaninis. We have always and without interruption sacrificed to the gods, and now in your presence in accordance with the edict's decree I have poured a libation, and made sacrifice, and partaken of the sacred victims. I request you to certify this for us below. Farewell.[5]

This is followed by the affidavit of the witnesses and the date. Of more than fifty such *libelli* now known none comes certainly from a Christian renegade, though we know such renegades existed, some actually sacrificing to the gods, and others pretending to and securing their certificates by bribery and fraud. The evidence of these documents is only indirect testimony to Christianity. Other official documents like deeds, receipts, contracts, census papers, petitions would have no occasion to indicate the Christianity of the persons involved.

Direct evidence to Christianity comes however in the letters beginning just about the same date. At least the ἐν κυρίῳ in a letter of Arrianus to Paulus is certainly decisive.[6] The name Paulus in this letter is of interest. For just about this time we get the first Christian names. They are at first only Peter and Paul. From the year 256, as Harnack reminds us, come our earliest synodical *acta*, those of North Africa. Among the 87 bishops voting there only two biblical names appear—Peter and Paul, and about the same time Dionysius of Alexandria writes, 'The children of the faithful are often called after Paul and also after Peter.'[7] But of course all this is much too late for the Book of Acts, and if I am to speak as promised for each culture of characteristic names I shall have to describe Christian names for the first centuries as non-existent. Gentiles converted did not change their own names, nor did Christian parents give distinctive Christian names to their children. It is just as well to remember this when for lack of any real information about the Theophilus to whom Acts is addressed, ancient or modern writers deal with the word as though it were a descriptive name, lover of God, applied playfully by the author to his patron, or adopted by the latter at a christening. It is a very common Greek name, no doubt the original name of a real person. I may add, though I would not press the point here, it is one of the Greek names most often used by Jews.[8] For several generations Christians named their children with names not significant of

Christianity, including names that were plainly Jewish or were even reminiscent of gods they certainly would not worship.

While therefore Christianity is not reflected in the letters and legal documents of Egypt before the year 250 another class of papyri has in very recent years been supplying even earlier evidence. These papyri are copies of Christian scriptures both canonical and uncanonical. The papyrus fragments of the gospels and other Christian writings discovered before 1930 could none of them have been dated before the middle of the third century but of more recent discoveries the dates set by scholars are continuously earlier and earlier. The large and important group of MSS. acquired by Sir Alfred Chester Beatty in the years 1930 and 1931 contains some pieces that are certainly either early or late second century. A fragment from a non-canonical Christian gospel connected with our canonical gospels was published in 1935.[9] This was two pieces of papyrus from Egypt then lately acquired in the British Museum. Its date, i.e., the date of actual MS. is the middle of the second century. And later in the same year there was published a papyrus which had long been lying in the John Rylands Library at Manchester. It contains only a very few verses of the Gospel of John (18 : 31-33; 37-38).[10] But it is dated in the first half of the second century. If that date remains unchallenged by palaeographers this fragment will prove to be (1) the oldest of any known pieces of Christian writing, (2) the oldest distinct evidence from any source for the existence of the Gospel of John and the new *terminus ad quem* for the much discussed question of its date, and (3) the earliest evidence of the presence of Christianity in Egypt.

The scantiness of extra-canonical evidence to early Christianity is not to be misunderstood. It is scarcely proof that Christianity did not exist, though such an argument from silence has been employed by those who wish to believe that Jesus of Nazareth was a mere myth. It means rather that Christianity or Christians as such did not get recorded. Paul testifies that in Corinth not many wise, not many mighty, not many noble had joined the church. If Erastus the treasurer of the city (ἀγορανόμος) and friend of Paul mentioned in Acts and Romans was one exception why should we expect him to be mentioned as a Christian in any non-Christian context, like the inscription lately found in a pavement at Corinth: 'Erastus, in appreciation of his appointment as aedile, laid the pavement at his own expense'?[11] Even the burial inscriptions of Christians long continued to bear the literally pagan abbreviation D.M., i.e., *Dis Manibus*, and why should we expect Roman historians or business documents to make obvious the private religious affiliation of the persons they mention unless it has some bearing on the matter in hand?

In this absence of contemporary explicit reference to Christianity in the apostolic age it may be worth while to discuss briefly four alleged echoes of it in non-Christian sources—one a passage long debated in an ancient author, the other three an inscription, a papyrus and some *graffiti* that have lately come to light. Three belong to the reign of Claudius, hence to the very heart of the period of history covered by Acts, the fourth either in that reign or the next.

1. The first is a single sentence in Suetonius' tersely written life of Claudius. *Iudaeos impulsore Chresto assidue tumultuantis Roma expulit.* 'The Jews he expelled from Rome . . . for continuously rioting.'[12] This item in Jewish history we have already noted. It agrees with a like statement in Acts 18 : 2, 'Claudius had commanded all the Jews to depart from Rome.' A later writer, Orosius,[13] claims to derive the same information from Josephus and dates it in the ninth year of Claudius (i.e., A.D. 49). There can be little doubt of the fact. But what of the two words we have omitted to translate, *impulsore Chresto*, 'Chrestus being the instigator (of their rioting).' It should be first remarked that Chrestus is a common Greek personal name, but that it is also a natural and frequent misspelling in *Christus* and especially *Christianus*. Now of course Jesus Christ was never in Rome, certainly not in the reign of Claudius. But it is probable that Christians were there in that reign, and while Suetonius writing two generations later has the matter confused, it is quite possible that Christian-Jewish conflicts were already occurring there and

have been somehow remembered as a reason for Claudius' strict action. To the Emperor, as to his proconsul in Achaia, Gallio, the quarrel might well seem as a purely domestic quarrel within Judaism 'about words and names and their own law', or, as another Roman official expresses it, 'disputes about the Jews' superstition and about one Jesus, who was dead, whom Paul affirmed to be alive.' To later Romans in the capital, acquainted with Christians or Chrestians as they called them, it was natural to suppose that Jewish-Christian disorders in the reign of Claudius had been instigated by the eponymous founder of what Suetonius calls in the next reign a new and baneful superstition.

2. In Alexandria also the reign of Claudius witnessed Jewish disorders. We know of these from several sources. But in 1924 was published from a papyrus found in the Egyptian Philadelphia a copy of a letter written to Alexandria by the Emperor Claudius in A.D. 41, the first year of his reign.[14] After rebuking the Alexandrines for molesting the Jews, long their fellow townsmen, in the exercise of their traditional worship and customs, the Emperor adds, 'and, on the other side, I bid the Jews not to busy themselves about anything beyond what they have held hitherto, and not henceforth as if you lived in two cities to send two embassies—a thing such as never occurred before now—nor to intrude into the gymnasiarchic and cosmetic games, but to profit by what they possess, and enjoy in a city not their own an abundance of all good things; and not to introduce or invite Jews who sail down to Alexandria from Syria or Egypt, thus compelling me to conceive the greater suspicion; otherwise I will by all means take vengeance on them as fomenting a general plague for the whole world.'

Now the Christians or Christ are not here mentioned by name. But more than one excellent scholar believes that behind the reference to 'two embassies (both Jewish) to Rome,' to 'Jews who sail from Syria to Alexandria' and 'the increasing suspicion and general plague for the whole world' is to be seen a new conflict within Alexandrian Judaism with more evident and more fanatical Mèssianic tendencies. This they explain as an incursion into that city, from Palestine proper or Antioch or other parts of the Roman province of Syria, of Jewish Christians with the gospel—perhaps those very Hellenists who were spread abroad in the persecution after the death of Stephen, together with like situations in other parts of the world as reported to the Emperor. Solomon Reinach called it 'the first allusion to Christianity in history', and independently G. de Sanctis declared, 'it is the earliest dated text, in which an allusion to Christianity occurs.'

3. The third item of possible indirect evidence to Christianity in the reign of Claudius is an imperial decree on the subject of violation of tombs. Though the inscription was discovered and brought to Paris as long ago as 1878 it was first published in 1930 by Franz Cumont in the *Revue Historique*.[15] Its date is not certain nor its meaning in all details. It is apparently a literal Greek translation of a Latin original rescript. Although other forms of desecration of burial are mentioned, the removal of the bodies by wicked guile is repeatedly condemned. It is equivalent to sacrilege against the gods. The Emperor concludes: 'Let it not be permitted for anyone to move a corpse at all. But if one does so, I wish him to be condemned to death on the charge of violation of burial.'

Now the striking things about this rescript are: the emphasis on removing bodies from tombs, the severity of the punishment, and above all the place of its supposed public erection and later discovery—Nazareth in Galilee. It is probable that a request had been made by a Roman procurator for an imperial judgment. Since Galilee first came under direct Roman control in A.D. 44 and since the lettering on the stone appears to belong not much if any later than the middle of the first century—the Caesar mentioned is very probably Claudius. Evidently the Roman official had had called to his attention a case of alleged removal of a corpse so that he consulted the highest authority about procedure. Equally severe punishment for such acts is not known to us to have been required at any period within the late Republic or early Empire. The act therefore seemed serious—those who remove corpses must be suppressed.

The conclusion reached by certain scholars is therefore this. In the Gospel of Matthew we read that the Jews accused the disciples of Jesus of having stolen the body of Jesus. This was their answer to the Christian claim that he had risen from the dead. It was part of the vigorous controversy between Jews and Christians, and although Matthew's Gospel was not written probably until later in the century, this story had doubtless had, as he says, long currency among the Jews 'until this day'.[16] The controversy between Jews and Christians was a disturbing element to Roman officials. According to our own Book of Acts it seemed to the procurator Festus to be due to certain differences of opinion about the Jews' own superstition and about a certain dead Jesus, whom Paul alleged to be alive. Now some scholars suppose that an earlier procurator or Emperor, accepting the Jewish story of Christian theft, hoped to suppress the difficulties by new measures. And so there was erected at Nazareth which was regarded as the fountain and source of the new religion—the sect of the Nazarenes—a copy of the Emperor's threat of punishment. It was doubtless a futile gesture and, so far as Christianity is concerned, due to a misunderstanding. But who will say that the first echoes of the gospel in secular history may not very well have been equally oblique and ill-founded?[17]

4. Another source of suggested early evidence of Christianity is in the many ossuaries, or rectangular burial urns found in the vicinity of Jerusalem and datable with all probability in the first Christian century. These limestone boxes to which the bones of the dead were removed to make room for new burials in the rock hewn sepulchres, either are plain or are decorated with rosettes in geometrical style, but they sometimes include markings scratched upon their surface with a sharp intrument or with paint or charcoal identifying by name the deceased. These names when they concur with names in Luke-Acts are useful as showing the currency of even the more unfamiliar names like Martha, Sapphira and Barsabbas. From time to time, however, it has been suggested that the combination of names indicates identity with actual New Testament characters. One cave found near Bethany in 1873 included among the Greek or Hebrew names of persons buried Martha, Eleazar (*Graece* Lazarus) and Mary. One of the sarcophagi with the name Sapphira is said to have been

found near another with the name Hananiah (i.e., Ananias). Another inscription has the exact combination 'Jesus son of Joseph'. These coincidences could be entirely ignored were it not for the fact that a cross is found marked on some of the ossuaries. It has been believed heretofore that the cross whether T shaped as the one on a wall at Herculaneum already mentioned, or with four arms of equal length as on the Jerusalem ossuaries, was not used as a Christian symbol until later centuries. My own opinion is that neither in Palestine nor in Italy should the cross any more than the names be associated in the first century with the followers of Jesus. Yet it was maintained by Prof. E. L. Sukenik that a chamber tomb which he excavated in 1945 in which occur such crosses on ossuaries, the name of Jesus followed by obscure words which he understands as cries of lament, and the name Barsabas found elsewhere he says only in the New Testament, viz. in Acts twice, a Joseph Barsabbas and a Judas Barsabbas, is the tomb of a Christian family of that name.[18]

I have recited at length the four alleged evidences of Christianity in non-canonical records of the apostolic age that readers may see for themselves how uncertain they are. There is not one of them on which the consensus of scholarly opinion accepts the Christian reference, though in each of them it has had the support of capable and unprejudiced historians. The important thing is that these are I believe absolutely all we have. Other discoveries may be hoped for, even if we regard that hope as improbable. For the apostolic age, as for the life of Jesus, we are dependent almost entirely on the Christian writings—and I may add—on the Christian writings of the canonical New Testament.

Space does not permit an analysis here of the Christian non-canonical references to the times of the apostles. The apocryphal books of Acts, beginning with the partly recovered *Acts of Peter*, probably add very little authentic knowledge of the apostolic age, or even confirmation of the information in our Book of Acts. It is mainly curiosity that leads one to quote from the *Acts of Paul and Thecla* the description of Paul's personal appearance as 'a man small in size, with meeting eyebrows, with a rather large nose, baldheaded, bowlegged, strongly built, full of grace, for at times he looked like a man and at times he had the face of an angel'. What these *Acts* do show is that fiction in the ancient world is often as full of accurate local colour and contemporary colour as is trustworthy history. The Greek and Roman novels may therefore be used both to confirm these colours and to warn us that accuracy in such details is not final proof of the historical accuracy of writings in other respects as well.[19]

The works of the church fathers from Clement of Rome to Eusebius though less inclined to sheer fiction than the apocrypha are equally unavailable to confirm or supplement the book of Acts. Most of their references to apostolic doings are of four kinds,—missionary labours, the founding of churches and of episcopal sees, the writing of scripture, and faithful martyrdom. Most of these events if genuine belong in date after the close of Acts. Many are assumptions based on hints in scripture itself or on general considerations. Few if any belong to an independent tradition of genuine history. Even the martyrdom of Peter and Paul at Rome under Nero has, when looked into, much less evidence than even Protestants suppose. Clement's First Epistle, usually regarded as the earliest writing outside the New Testament, is characteristically vague about such an outcome. I quote the well known passage in his list of victims of jealousy:

But to cease from the examples of old time, let us come to those who contended in the days nearest to us; let us take the noble examples of our own generation. Because of jealousy and envy the greatest and most righteous pillars were persecuted and contended unto death. Let us set before our eyes the good apostles: Peter who because of unrighteous jealousy suffered not one or two but many labours, and having thus given his testimony went to the glorious place which was his due.

Because of jealousy and strife Paul showed the way to the prize of endurance; seven times he was in bonds, he was exiled, he was stoned, he was a herald both in the East and in the West, he gained the noble fame of his faith, he taught righteousness to all the world, and when he had reached the limits of the West he gave his testimony before the rulers and thus passed from the world and was taken up into the Holy Place, having become the greatest example of endurance.[20]

Such rhetoric with its 'not one or two but many labours', its 'seven times', its 'limits of the West' and its 'gave his testimony' cannot be reduced to definite history.

Geographical data about Christianity in the apostolic age are as little expanded by sources beyond Acts and the Pauline letters as are biographical data. First Peter, the Book of Revelation and the letters of Ignatius imply Christianity in certain cities in the province of Asia and in certain other provinces in Asia Minor, for which neither Acts nor Paul bears witness. The writings are probably all later in date, though the presence of Christianity may be older in the districts they mention. The Asian cities are Smyrna, Pergamum, Thyatira, Sardis, Philadelphia, Magnesia, Tralles; the districts: Cappadocia, Bithynia and Pontus. For the last of these we have the correspondence of Pliny and Trajan of the year A.D. 112-113, in which reference is made to Christianity in Bithynia or more likely Pontus not merely in his own time but some twenty five years earlier. It is noteworthy that Ramsay is inclined to place the origins of Christianity in these areas outside the province of Asia as no earlier than the end of Acts, and that Harnack in listing places where Christianity is known to have existed before the end of the century can add only one to those already mentioned, and that by inference, Alexandria.[21] That shows how little non-Christian and non-canonical sources add to our knowledge of the expansion of Christianity in the apostolic age.

It would be wrong however to suppose that Acts makes any claim to geographical completeness. Take the province of Asia. Though Acts mentions Christians only at Ephesus and Troas, it says that all who dwelt in Asia heard the word of the Lord. We learn already from Paul's letters of other churches in the province which he had not seen, Colossae, Laodicea and Hierapolis.[22] In other places Acts takes for granted Christian communities without telling how they came to be. Damascus is one example, Rome another, Puteoli another. These were what Paul regarded as other men's foundations, and it is largely because Acts like Paul limits itself to areas of Paul's labours that the origin of these churches is not told in that book.

It is important to recall these circumstances in dealing with the references in pagan sources which we considered above, far-fetched and uncertain as they are. They have to do with Christianity in the reign of Claudius in places, where, even without their testimony, we should have to assume its existence anyhow. Of two of those places we have already spoken—Egypt and Rome. The third is even more interesting, Galilee. It is a striking fact that we know so little of Christianity in Galilee. In Acts Jerusalem and then Antioch seem to become the centre of the movement. Only once (9:31) in summary fashion does the book refer to the church in all Judea and Galilee and Samaria. Down to Eusebius there is no reference to Galilean Christians. But the resurrection stories in the other gospels than Luke's and particularly Paul's statement (1 Cor. 15:6) that Jesus appeared to above five hundred brethren at one time seem to imply an early persistence in Galilee of Jesus' followers. It has been urged that the tradition which associated the resurrection appearances of Jesus with Galilee, found in Mark, Matthew and the appendix of John 21, is testimony to the existence or continuance in that area of a Christian community. More lasting evidence though less tangible seems to me the actual contents of our gospels, especially such material as is usually assigned to Q. This material has had a long oral history, and part of that seems to belong neither in Judea nor in the mission field but in Galilee.

The recent study of the Gospels is making clear to us how important for our understanding of them it would be to know thoroughly the apostolic age. They are not mere uncoloured accounts of Jesus' words and deeds. But they have included the interests, motives and ideas of the generation through which the story had already been handed down—largely in a fluid state of oral tradition. They are at once a witness to that early Christianity and they themselves are in need of being corrected or discounted by that Christianity if the facts and the figure behind them are to be surely known. Now the Book of Acts is our principal narrative source for knowledge of that exact period in which these influences on the gospel material were active.

Still more important is the Book of Acts for understanding Paul's letters. A narrative of Paul's life would be almost impossible without it. We might, to be sure, collect from the Epistles some data about Paul—his Jewish birth, his Pharisaic training, his early hostility to Christianity, his active preaching of the gospel from Jerusalem round about to Illyricum. These and many minor data are to be gleaned from the Epistles, and as first hand autobiographical data they are of great historical value; but they are mere fragments unarranged and without the meaning that they receive when fitted into the framework of Acts. Acts is to Paul's letters what Mark is to Q,—in fact, what biography usually is to letters, what history is to literature.

But the relation is one of mutual illumination, and our problem here is not what Acts contributes to our understanding of other Christian sources but what they contribute to the understanding of Acts. Whatever the Gospels tell us trustworthily about the life and teaching of Jesus they are still more to be trusted, so far as they go, in their undesigned disclosure of thought in the apostolic age. As a source they may be used to supplement, confirm or correct the Book of Acts. As for the relationship between the Epistles of Paul and Acts, this was made the subject of an important little study called *Horae Paulinae* by William Paley, author of the once famous Paley's *Evidences*. His motive in this historical work was also apologetic. He wished to confirm the reliability of both the letters and Acts by what he called 'undesigned coincidences'. Taking the reasonable view that two independent and truthful witnesses are bound, where they do not positively overlap, to provide supplementary and reconcilable statements, Paley ingeniously listed a large number of such coincidences. This dovetailing has of course been done by others before and since, and it might well be undertaken by anybody just for his own amusement. To the puzzle addict it detracts very little from his pleasure that someone else has seen before him how neatly the pieces fit each other.

Paley was justified in feeling reassured by his experiments.

I

There is little doubt in my mind that the author of Acts did not know the extant Epistles or if he did that he made little use of them. The coincidences are therefore genuinely independent and undesigned. They agree as two sober and independent documents should and often do agree. The differences—while some of them are more serious and must be dealt with more ingenuously than ingeniously—are in many cases no reflection on the good faith of either writer. It is true for example that the vehicle in which Paul made his escape over the wall of Damascus is different in the two writings—two Greek words as different perhaps as a bag is different from a basket. But the other data given in the two accounts though they are not the same, and though they are mentioned in quite different settings are rather supplementary than contradictory.[23]

As an example of the relation we may take Paul's last journey from Greece to Jerusalem. The motives of the journey Acts nowhere betrays, though it is repeatedly made clear that they are regarded as significant. It begins or ends with ceremonies of the nature of a vow (18 : 18; 21 : 23-26). It is carried out with haste (18 : 21, 22) and urgent desire to be in Jerusalem by Pentecost (20 : 16), and it is marked by forebodings of what will happen and does happen to Paul upon his arrival. Furthermore Acts lists in one passage (20 : 4) the large and geographically representative personnel of the party. Beside Paul and the unnamed speaker in the 'we' (traditionally Luke), they are Sopater, Aristarchus, Secundus, Gaius, Timothy, Tychicus and Trophimus.

Now the letters of Paul, especially chapter fifteen of Romans, make unmistakably clear what this is all about. Paul has for years been collecting a fund—Near East Relief—for the 'saints' at Jerusalem. Various churches have appointed delegates, though these are nowhere named in the letter, and now as he writes Paul is going up with them from Corinth to Jerusalem. There is in Romans the same foreboding fear of what may happen to Paul. To that extent it overlaps with Acts and further, though the last chapter of Romans may not belong just here and does not speak of them as travelling with Paul, it mentions as with him: Timothy, Lucius, Jason, Sosipater, Tertius, Gaius, Erastus and

Quartus, four of whom may be identical with the Timothy, Lucas, Sopater and Gaius of the delegation in Acts.

In fact one of the coincidences between the Epistles and the Acts is just this repetition of names. I think it is fair to say that three-quarters of the persons associated with Paul in Acts reappear in the epistles or at least persons of the same names. The list just mentioned from Romans includes two more names that occur in Acts, Erastus and Jason; while of the preceding list from Acts, Aristarchus, Tychicus and Trophimus appear in other Epistles. Conspicuous in both letters and Acts are further Silas (Silvanus), Barnabas, Apollos, Prisca and Aquila. The wife in the last named couple it is true is called by Paul consistently Prisca and in Acts consistently Priscilla, but this difference is more than offset by the fact that in each of the two writings she is mentioned two out of three times in the unconventional order—preceding her husband.

At Corinth Acts tells us that Crispus the ruler of the synagogue believed and that Sosthenes another ruler of the synagogue was beaten up in a riot at the Roman proconsul's judgment seat. Our First Corinthians begins as written by 'Paul . . . and Sosthenes our brother'[24] and shortly thereafter we read, 'I thank God that I baptized none of you save Crispus and Gaius.'

Even in Paul's own name there is a coincidence not mentioned by Paley. It is Acts alone who gives us his Jewish name, Saul. It is only from Paul's letters (Romans and Philippians) that we learn that he was of the tribe of Benjamin, and no doubt named for King Saul, the most famous previous member of that tribe, whom indeed Acts elsewhere so describes (13 : 21).

Paley has many ingenious combinations, most of them quite fair and convincing, though too long to retail here. Here is another family relationship of interest. Acts tells us that Paul and Barnabas quarrelled and finally separated because the latter would and the former would not take John Mark with them on their next missionary journey. Paul's reasons are given in Acts but not those of Barnabas. Perhaps Paul himself gives a clue in a letter (Col. 4 : 10) when he refers to Mark a cousin of Barnabas.

Much has happened in New Testament criticism since 1790 when William Paley published at Dublin the first edition of this work. And a new *Horae Paulinae* would have to compare Acts with the Epistles especially in the light of the new theories about the latter. Not all these theories are proved, but neither were the traditional assumptions about the date, place, unity or genuineness of the letters upon which Paley relied. I need scarcely remind you how fully these new theories cover the Pauline corpus. They suggest:

That Romans and Ephesians were once circular letters intended at least partly for other readers.

That the last chapter of Romans was separate and addressed to Ephesus.

That Second Corinthians contains parts of two letters and that the same may be true of First Corinthians and Philippians as well as Romans.

That Galatians was written to the churches of Antioch, Iconium, Lystra and Derbe and not to the Galatians in the stricter ethnic sense living in the northern part of the province of the same name.

That Philemon, Colossians, Ephesians, and Philippians were written not from a Roman imprisonment of Paul but one or all of them from an earlier imprisonment in Ephesus.

That First and Second Thessalonians were written and dispatched to the readers in the reverse order.

That the Pastoral Epistles, usually attributed to Paul's life after Acts leaves him, are not genuine as a whole but may contain genuine fragments belonging in the earlier period of Paul's life that Acts does cover.

Such new theories if adopted create no new difficulties in Acts, they rather supply new opportunities for the puzzle fitter's art. How Paley would have rejoiced to think that the greetings to Prisca and Aquila in Romans 16 were sent not to the Rome whence that much-travelled couple had been expelled but precisely as we can now believe to Ephesus where Acts has last brought them; or that the Galatians whom Paul reminds, 'Ye received me as a messenger of God,' included precisely those people of Lystra who undertook to offer him sacrifice as being

Hermes himself; or that the visit to the Philippians projected in Paul's letter to them was planned when in prison in Ephesus not at Rome and that both its fulfilment and the earlier dispatch of Timothy to Philippi also promised in the letter are actually recorded in Acts 20 : 1 and 19 : 22 respectively. The relations to Acts of possible genuine fragments in Second Timothy constitute a most delightful enigma.

But the Epistles of Paul do not everywhere give such confirming impressions of the accuracy of Acts. Of course there are many evidences of the incompleteness of Acts. Though it mentions many of Paul's companions, Titus, who plays such an important part in Second Corinthians and Galatians is not mentioned at all, at least by that name. Though Acts mentions much of Paul's missionary work it has no specific allusion as has Paul to Illyricum or to Arabia. Though it mentions many vicissitudes of Paul's life, the list of them appearing in Second Corinthians 11 is very much larger. Of the more definite adventures there listed— five Jewish and three Roman beatings, one stoning, three shipwrecks, twenty-four hours drifting in the open sea, and a flight over the wall at Damascus,—thirteen items in all, only three are plainly found in Acts up to that point—one Roman beating, one stoning and the flight from Damascus. Of course this merely shows the incompleteness of Acts, where incompleteness is quite pardonable. The situation would have been more embarrassing if Acts had mentioned more instances than Paul did, instead of vice versa, say two stonings instead of one, and in fact Paley points out with satisfaction that Acts comes so close to a second stoning as to describe an attempt of Jews and Greeks to stone Paul and Barnabas at Iconium but adds, 'they became aware of it and fled unto the cities of Lycaonia, Lystra and Derbe, and the region round about.'

The apparent discrepancies between Acts and Paul's letters have often been discussed. They are painfully familiar to every theological student who has had to deal with Galatians. They played a large part in the Tübingen theory of early Christian tendencies—a theory of which, as of other theories, the débris tends to remain long after the main structure has fallen. It is quite possible that the author of Acts is more accurate about local details than about the exact course of the major units in Paul's life —what we call his missionary journeys and his visits to Jerusalem. He might well have got the order wrong, transferred a feature from one visit to another. Even a participant could have done so. In connection with the accuracy and authorship of Acts it is asked further whether the description of speaking with tongues at Pentecost can be reconciled with the account in First Corinthians, whether the circumcising of Timothy at Derbe and the association in a Jewish vow at Jerusalem can be believed of such a critic of law observance as Paul shows himself in Galatians, and whether either his own independence or his ideals of freedom from the Law for his own churches would have allowed him to accept the so-called decrees on meat offered to idols and other matters.

Now there is no reason to suppose that our writer perfectly sensed the mind of Paul—and who did so sense it, either in his own day or since? We cannot be sure that the author of Acts does not occasionally, in spite of other most reliable data, misreport not merely the words but even the acts and attitudes of his hero. There are reasons to prefer Paul's own words when such choices must be made. But the non-Pauline traits of Acts are not so much intentional misrepresentation, but only the reflection of other currents in the early church contemporary at least with the writer, and perhaps with the events that he records. To this non-Pauline element in Acts I must now turn.

It is not only by the very individual Christianity of Paul that Acts must be tested, but also by the contemporary non-Pauline Christianity. Our gross ignorance of these other lines of the apostolic age makes us forget them and in any case the task of comparison is a delicate one involving many subjective judgments; but in conclusion it must be at least sketched.

The early church was a movement prior to Paul and later than Paul and apart from him in his lifetime. We know very little of it directly from early sources, but we can be sure it existed. What it was like we infer from what it later developed into rather than from contemporary documents, for I am persuaded that neither the speeches of Peter and James in Acts nor the epistles in the New Testament that bear their names are any more contemporary to the Apostles' time than are either the Pauline speeches in Acts or the deutero-Pauline epistles. This non-Pauline Christianity, how-ever, to be reconstructed from these and other later products, is nevertheless the very environment against which we should, if we could, test the Book of Acts. Its earliest and least known period is the background of the events in Acts, its later and better known phase is contemporary with the author of Acts, its latest and best known phase is catholic Christianity which marks the culmination of tendencies at work in the earlier period. What kind of begin-nings, we may ask, had such a Christian outcome, and does the picture in the Book of Acts fit into such a reconstructed history? I can only note, briefly each, a few such correspondences.

Early Christianity—to judge from results—must have had a strong missionary impulse. There must have been an urgency to preach it, as well as the influence of contagion and spontaneous dissemination. The Gospels themselves confirm this view by the urgency in their teaching of Jesus. They give us a picture of hurried evangelization by the Twelve or the Seventy. The Book of Acts agrees in its picture of activity, urgency and the almost miraculous triumph over obstacles. Even the apocalyptic element is not absent in the speeches of Acts.

Early Christianity must have emphasized the resurrection of Christ, as again do the speeches of Acts. Paul too emphasized it, but the death of Christ plays a more important part in his letters and in some later Christianity than in either Luke or Acts. From this two volume work the atonement motifs of Isaiah 53 are conspicuously lacking. But to what must have played a more universal part in the founding of the church—the resurrection of Jesus—the evangelist seems quite faithful.

Early Christianity did not all forsake Judaism to the extent that Paul sometimes seems to do in his letters. The Book of Acts pictures a church growing naturally in the bosom of Judaism without going the lengths of Paul's opponents.

The Old Testament must have played a large part in the earliest Christian preaching to Jews. We have of course no actual sermons from that period but we can infer the importance of prophecy from later indications. The sermons in Acts, though they may be no more than editorial compositions, are nevertheless excellent reflections of the probable use of scripture in the earliest period.

The Old Testament was used not only on behalf of the Christians but against the Jews. In their bold appropriation of their opponent's heritage this was one of the most astonishing of the early Christian manoeuvres. It had its antecedents no doubt in the Jewish critique of tendencies among themselves. We find it in Paul and elsewhere in the New Testament. But it is most conspicuous in the Book of Acts.

The speech of Stephen represents not only this but another aspect of early Christian use of the Old Testament—what we may call its Alexandrian use. Allegory and typology of this sort are far more characteristic of later Christian writings than they are of the canonical ones. There is a distinct difference between the typological use of the Old Testament in the Epistle of Barnabas, the Preaching of Peter, and the Clementines and its use in the synoptic Gospels or in Paul. Now as Professor Bacon has clearly shown, this use represents the closest affinity we have to the argument and method of Stephen's speech. What that speech shows is merely an early example of a scriptural usage that later times abundantly attest.[25]

How far the speeches in Acts[26] are accurate reports of speeches actually delivered is a disputed question. They may be merely, like the speeches of Thucydides, the historian's own composition, his dramatic imagination of what the actors were likely to have said. They are at least a testimony to Christianity no later than the author's own time and are none the less useful as a mark of first-century, if not the most primitive, Christian thought. It makes little difference for our present purpose whether they represent the ideas of Peter and Stephen, or the ideas of Luke and his time. Perhaps they represent what Luke thought the ideas of Peter and Stephen had been. In any case they attest a relatively early and non-Pauline strand of Christianity and are attested by what our other sources suggest to us of the non-Pauline development.

The Book of Acts also attests the influence of Paul. Its author was evidently an admirer of the apostle and an early witness to his importance. He would not otherwise have devoted to him so large a part of his history. Now the influence of Paul in the first century, and indeed in the second, is by no means uniform or unquestioned. To judge only from our other New Testament writings it was largely negligible. Hebrews and Revelation show I think almost no knowledge of Paul or effect of his influence. I doubt whether it is visible really in any of our four Gospels, though it has often been claimed for at least three of them. In the Epistle of James Paul's view of faith and works is at most contradicted, while Second Peter, the very late interloper in our canon, though it may not positively slight 'the wisdom given to' 'our beloved brother Paul', is more impressed by the obscurity and consequent misuse of the contents of Paul's epistles.

The best real evidence the New Testament gives of the post mortem appreciation of Paul is not anything it says but its very contents, its witness to the collecting and transmission to posterity of his epistles. Whether this attention to his memory is actually due to Acts as Professor Goodspeed thinks, or whether they are independent witnesses to his influence and esteem in Christendom, the collection of Paul's epistles and the composition of the Book of Acts are certainly nearly contemporary in date and sympathetic in tendency. The collector of Paul's epistles may never have read Acts, and the author of Paul's biography may never have read his epistles. But they both reflect the same background,—the reverence for his memory.

Associated with Paul in Acts is the apostle Peter. He is without doubt the next most conspicuous figure in the volume, and the conscious parallelism between the two apostles is not merely a modern imagination. For the author they were in fact and in thought parallel. Now I am not denying the historical importance of Peter in early Christianity. There are reasons outside of Acts for assigning him a like prominence, especially as an early witness and herald of the resurrection of Jesus. But that such significance should be guaranteed in later tradition and that Peter should in memory become with Paul the two pillars of the church was not inevitable. Yet every later reference to Paul shows that just this occurred. Again and again in subsequent Christian literature the two are mentioned side by side. The passage from First Clement has been quoted. The reference to Paul in Second Peter is much the same since it is Peter himself that professes to be writing. 'I do not,' writes Ignatius in his epistle to Rome, 'I do not order you as did Peter and Paul.' The same combination continues on down through the centuries. Quite early we have the tradition that even 'in their death they were not divided'. The beginnings of this parallelism were doubtless found even in their own lifetime[27] but Acts is the next oldest witness to its continuance and development.

Very much the same comment may be made about the leadership of apostles. The term apostolic is not an unambiguous one but in an accepted sense became ultimately the imprimatur of catholic Christianity. Paul's letters show in part an acceptance and in part a revolt from the supremacy of the Twelve, while the genius of the kind of worship that he implies certainly gives them no direct or indirect control of leadership in that area. Now Acts says relatively little about the apostles and worship and indeed very little about church organization in general. We may note however not merely the elders at Jerusalem, the leadership of James there, and the story of a formal council there with written decrees (sic), but frequently in the book the evidence of an incipient, as it seems to us now though not to the writer, apostolic authority. Pains are taken to fill out the number of the Twelve or to relieve them of unnecessary secular tasks. They form in Jerusalem a central authority, remaining there in spite of persecution, and confirming the results of other men's labours afield whether with Samaritans, with a devout Roman at Caesarea, or with sheer Gentiles at Antioch or in Asia Minor. Whether with some we should claim that such eminence of the Twelve goes back to Jesus' own lifetime, or whether we regard it rather as a later evolution, it is already partly present in Acts and for the author's time at least it is a significant item in his Christian environment destined to grow to extreme proportions in the days to follow.

The external Christian evidence by which one can test Acts proves in general to be rather scanty, and our effort in this chapter is a good deal like an attempt to test by other evidence for the character of Samuel Johnson that incomparable picture by James Boswell. Except for the narrative or personal references in the letters of Paul the only area in which Acts finds much contemporary Christianity for comparison is in the matter of theology. And here one must handle the question with great caution. Yet the speeches and other features of the book fit well that general development of Christian thought, practice, or organization which we partly witness in nearly contemporary documents and partly infer from the later results of that development. For the later development itself however the Book of Acts becomes something more. It becomes itself a formative factor.

At this point however, the Christianity subsequent to Acts cannot be used as attesting quite independently the development parallel to Acts. In the growth of apostolicity as a standard, in the more formal organization of the church, in the respect for the Apostle Paul, in the assurance of the church of its divine credentials and divine mission, the Book of Acts, once it was written, becomes a formative factor. Its influence has extended from that day to this. And so as we conclude our fivefold sketch of the Book of Acts in contemporary history, an inviting door is opened to another subject, the Book of Acts in subsequent history.

NOTES TO CHAPTER V

1. A convenient collection of these and later passages with good bibliography is W. den Boer, *Scriptorum Paganorum I-IV Saec. de Christianis Testimonia* (Textus Minores ii), Leiden, 1948.

2. Cf. .A. Mauri, La Croce di Ercolano, *Atti della Pontificia Accademia Romana di Archeologia, Rendiconti* 15, 1939, 193-218. Were one to see such a phenomenon in the ruins of a modern city one would guess that it indicated a place on a plastered wall where once had been a shelf supported by a middle bracket.

3. The state of discussion of this acrostic was well summarized by Hugh Last in *Journal of Theological Studies*, N.S., vol. 3, 1952, 92-97, The Rotas-Sator Square: Present Position and Future Prospects. For bibliography rather than an acceptable solution see Harald Fuchs, Die Herkunft der Satorformel, *Schweizerisches Archiv für Volkskunde*, 47, 1951, 28-54. Cf. S. Eitrem who in

Eranos 48, 1950, 73 f, holds the pagan origin of the palindrome. Otherwise one would have to regard this Pompeii evidence (there are two cases of the acrostic in Pompeii), either as made later by early visitors to the ruins or as the most ancient Christian inscription known and the first which establishes existence of Latin Christianity, as Cumont did in 1927. But see the shrewd remarks of C. H. Kraeling in *Crozer Quarterly*, 22, 1945, pp. 28-38.

4. Cf. H. I. Bell, Evidences of Christianity in Egypt during the Roman Period, in *Harvard Theological Review*, 37, 1944, pp. 185-208. The same writer has returned to the subject later, e.g., in his *Cults and Creeds in Graeco-Roman Egypt*, 1953, Lecture IV.

5. Cited from John R. Knipfing, The Libelli of the Decian Persecution, *Harvard Theological Review*, 16, 1923, p. 386; revised after Winter, *op. cit.*, p. 140. Cf. R. Roasenda, Decio e i libellatici, *Didaskaleion*, 5, 1927, pp. 31-68.

6. P. Bas. 16. G. Ghedini, *Lettere cristiane*, 1923, p. 3, cited in Winter, *op. cit.*, p. 144, in his chapter on 'Evidences of Christianity in the Private Letters.'

7. Harnack, *Mission and Expansion of Christianity*, English Translation, Second Edition, 1908, p. 423, citing Cyprian's works and p. 426 citing Eusebius *H.E.*, vii, 25, 14.

8. V. Tcherikover, *The Jews in Egypt in the Hellenistic-Roman Age in the Light of the Papyri*, Jerusalem, 1945, p. 2: 'Among the Greek names we note the theophoric names Dositheos, Dorotheos, Theophilos, etc., as being widely spread among the Jews; yet it would be false to consider every man named Theophilos a Jew.' Cf. p. 29, and pp. 241-243 of the Hebrew text.

9. H. I. Bell and T. C. Skeat, *Fragments of an Unknown Gospel*, 1935.

10. C. H. Roberts, *An Unpublished Fragment of the Fourth Gospel*, Manchester, 1935.

11. See note 26 on p. 55.

12. Suetonius, *Claudius*, 25, 4. On the explicit reference in Tacitus to Christians in Rome under Nero see two more recent discussions, both under the title, Tacitus über die Christen, by Harold Fuchs in *Vigiliae Christianae*, 4, 1950, 65-93, and by Karl Büchner in *Aegyptus*, 33, 1953, 181-192.

13. vii, 6, 15. This date fits the reference in Acts 18 : 2 very well according to the usual chronology assigned to Acts. See *Beginnings of Christianity*, v, p. 459. But much can be said for dating the expulsion earlier in about A.D. 41, the first year of Claudius' reign. This would be a natural inference from the reference in Suetonius. It would account for the absence of any reference to the event in our text of Tacitus' *Annales*, since his account of the years 37 to 47 is missing. Such a date would make any reference to Christians in the passage more unlikely. Yet H. Janne who vigorously espouses the early date thinks that definitely Christian disturbance is implied almost simultaneously at Rome ('Impulsore Chresto', *Annuaire de l'Institut de Philologie et d'Histoire Orientales et Slaves*, 2, 1933-34, pp. 531-553), at Alexandria by Claudius' letter mentioned below, by the decrees of Caesar mentioned at Thessalonica in Acts 17: 7, and at Antioch by some references to trouble there in Josephus ('La Lettre de Claude,' etc., *ibid.*, 4, 1936, pp. 273-295).

14. H. I. Bell, *Jews and Christians in Egypt*, 1924, pp. 1-37 (P. Lond. 1912).

15. Vol. 163, pp. 241-266. It was published officially by Louis Robert, *Collection Froehner, Inscriptions Grecques*, Paris, 1936, 114 f. See the mono-

graphs entitled *Diatagma Kaisaros* by Stephan Lösch, Freiburg, 1936, and Hieronymus Markowski, 1937, and the review of them by A. D. Nock in the *American Journal of Philology*, 60, 1939, 118-122. For the abundant early bibliography see Lösch, *op. cit.*, pp. xi ff., and Johannes Irmscher, *Zeitschrift für die neutestamentliche Wissenschaft*, 52, 1949, pp. 173 f. For a wider context cf. Andre Parrot, *Malédictions et Violations de Tombes*, Paris, 1939 and the review by A. D. Nock in *Journal of Biblical Literature*, 60, 1941, pp. 88-95, and Erich Gerner, Tymborychia, *Zeitschrift der Savigny-Stiftung*, Rom. Abt. LXI, 1941, pp. 230-275, supplementing his article of the same title in Pauly-Wissowa.

16. Matt. 28: 15. Justin Martyr, *Dial.*, 108, 2, repeats the Jewish charge, but is probably dependent on Matthew.

17. Unfortunately it is only known that the inscription was acquired at Nazareth, not that it was found there or originally erected there. In the 1870's Nazareth was a natural market for dealers in antiquities.

18. E. L. Sukenik, The Earliest Records of Christianity, *American Journal of Archaeology*, vol. 51, 1947, pp. 351-365. Of the earlier literature it will be sufficient to mention two negative articles: L. H. Vincent, *Atti della Pontificia Accademia Romana di Archeologia*, Rendiconti 7, 1932, pp. 215-239. C. H. Kraeling, *The Biblical Archaeologist*, vol. 9, 1946, pp. 16-20. Cf. H. L. Jansen, *Symbolae Osloenses*, Fasc. 28, 1950, pp. 109-110. The word ἰοῦ interpreted as 'woe!' is as uncertain as the interpretation of the two crossed lines as a cross. For alternatives see S. Eitrem, Notes on Demonology in the New Testament (*Symbolae Osloenses*, Fasc. Supplet. XII), 1950, p. 11.

19. For a delightful account of such literature see *Some Ancient Novels*, by F. A. Todd, London, 1940.

20. 1 Clement 5.

21. Harnack, *Mission* (all editions, Book IV, chapter iii, part i). For Alexandria the Western text of Acts 18: 25 explicitly and the other text perhaps implicitly imply that Christianity was known in Alexandria about A.D. 50. Cf. *Beginnings*, vols. iii and iv, *ad loc.*

22. Colossians 2: 1, cf. 4: 13.

23. Acts 9: 23-25; 2 Cor. 11: 32-33. Cf. above pp. 19-21.

24. Acts 18: 17 does not suggest that Sosthenes was a Christian, and it would be possible to deny the identity of the persons so named. The *Monumenta Asiae Minoris Antiquae*, vols. 4 and 6, Index, *s.v.*, indicate that at some times and places the name Sosthenes was relatively common.

25. For one feature of Stephen's speech see above, pp. 105-106. For attempts to place it theologically in early Christianity see B. W. Bacon in *Biblical and Semitic Studies*, by members of the Semitic and Biblical Faculty of Yale University, 1902, pp. 213-276; M. Simon, Saint Stephen and the Jerusalem Temple, *Journal of Ecclesiastical History*, 2, 1951, pp. 127-142, and the larger works by himself and by H. J. Schoeps to which Simon there refers.

26. Of recent literature on the speeches in Acts nothing surpasses the essay by Martin Dibelius presented to the Heidelberg Academy in 1944, printed in its *Sitzungsberichte* in 1949 and reprinted in his *Aufsätze zur Apostelgeschichte*, 1951, pp. 120-162.

27. Gal. 2: 7-8; cf. 1 Cor. 1: 12; 9: 5; 15: 5, 8.

CHAPTER VI

SUBSEQUENT HISTORY

The preceding chapters have dealt with the historic cultural situation which surrounded the Book of Acts. The ambiguity of our general title permits us to include now a quite different story, more intimately associated with the book itself: its own history. There is history in the book, but there is also history *of* the book. 'Habent sua fata libelli.'[1] A segment of this history is the subject of the present chapter.

The larger scope of this topic permits even its division into two fairly obvious sections, one in a sense preceding and preconditioning the actual writing, and one succeeding it. Elsewhere I have written somewhat fully on the former. Recognizing the unity of both volumes to Theophilus, I considered in turn the chief formative factors in the making of Luke-Acts,—the materials, the common methods, the personality of the author, and his purpose.[2] The latter has to do with the factors affecting the Book of Acts, once it was written, and also with the rôle it has played and the influence it has had from that day to this.

One curious fact should be mentioned that is true of both these two divisions of the book's existence. The identification of the author and of the date and place of writing makes very little difference to either discussion. The formative factors could be extensively studied without even raising the questions when? where? and by whom?[3] For the factors themselves determined the contents. They explain the book's character very largely. One hardly need know who, when or where if one knows what was written and how and why. There is a finality to it, so that we can add to Pilate's famous phrase, 'What I have written, I have written,' similar self-evident statements, 'Whoever has written, has written,' and whenever and wherever as well.

Likewise, as far as we can now see, the facts of authorship, date and provenience had very little influence on the subsequent history of the book. One does not know how far they were known. Its history would have been much the same if a different unidentified author had written the same book at a somewhat different time or place. The contents of the book affected and was affected by later developments, and if ideas about date, place and authorship entered in, their influence was not dependent on the truth of the ideas about origins, but on their being held.

Thus the history of this book, and indeed of many other books, rests primarily upon its contents and secondarily upon ideas entertained about its origin; but it rests almost not at all upon the actual facts of origin. The ideas of origin have influence and the contents have influence. We can study the subsequent history of Acts as we can study its prior history without settling these often emphasized questions. They are questions that have been raised in the past and in the present in connection with quite other interests, such as inspiration, orthodoxy and historical value.

The segment of subsequent history which we shall canvass is one which is also somewhat obscure. For in the first generations Acts is little mentioned. We infer what happened largely by still later evidence rather than by any contemporary knowledge. This is about equally true of other New Testament books, but here we concentrate attention on Acts. The book itself tells much of its own history up to the time it was written. After that we are in the dark, as in a tunnel, and emerge only late and partially. Our subject is the early and unrecorded history of Acts.

The beginning, or *terminus a quo* of this segment of history is not defined by any calendar year. Just how even without attempting to fix a date shall we describe the event or era from which we use the term 'later history'? There is no real reason to suppose the author wrote or even planned a third volume.[4] But good scholars have supposed he did. In that case would the publication of Acts have waited for it? In any case did the publication of Luke wait while Acts was in preparation? It has been suggested that even Acts was not quite finished.[5] Even if it was normally published that would not be quite as definite an event as with a modern book. At most it would be more like a 'release' in modern newspaper terminology.[6]

The double work, Luke and Acts, was written for publication. It was not a private memorandum. The address to the individual Theophilus indicates that just the reverse of an individual audience was contemplated. Books without dedication or preface may also have aimed at or secured a general circulation. The presence of those literary features merely assures us that from the start Luke and Acts were so intended. The effect on Theophilus himself was not the main concern of the author, and we of course do not know what that effect was. What we do know is that the books got some circulation. The autograph copy has now perished but not before it was copied. Books intended to be copied should conform to the customary limits of length. If the original was not too long for the usual length scroll its reproduction was feasible. It has been estimated that if written in a hand with columns like those on Codex Vaticanus the Book of Acts would have required a roll of 31 or 32 feet in length.[7] Since the Gospel of Luke is within three per cent of the same length, the author has made possible the reproduction of both books on rolls of the same standard of length. It is safe to assume that as long as scrolls were commonly employed, scrolls of this length were obtainable. Another book requiring about the same space for copying is the Gospel of Matthew.

When writing standards change the restrictions placed upon arrangement by the conventional scope of the commercial materials for writing also change. Possibly the use of scrolls made of skins of leather or parchment once preceded the use of scrolls of papyrus or succeeded it or was parallel with it. We assume that papyrus was the material used by the New Testament writers. The Old Testament books translated into Greek took much more space than when written in Hebrew. The larger ones were therefore divided into two parts—as we note in the case of Samuel, Kings and Chronicles. There is some evidence that for purposes of translation other Old Testament books were divided in half in the sense of having the two halves translated by separate translators. And the books when translated into Greek were sometimes divided and entrusted to different Greek scribes to copy. There is some evidence, also, of classical books divided into two by editors or even authors.[8] Luke and Acts, however, seem to belong to that quite common situation where the original author, owing to recognized restrictions in scrolls, arranged his material in parts of equal size as separate volumes.

This habit and necessity of putting parts of the same work in physically separate units, no matter how carefully the text of each volume marks its position in the series, leads inevitably to separation. What librarian or dealer in old books today is not pestered by the presence of isolated volumes of two volume works? Fortunately our author had the judgment or foresight to make each of his two volumes somewhat self-sufficient, though in doing so he has perhaps prevented some modern readers from recognizing their fundamental unity. Ancient conditions and practices being what they were, there is no reason now to regard Acts as a mere afterthought or sequel, or to suppose that the preface of the Gospel was intended for less than the whole work.

In addition to the fact of physical separateness other factors contributed to the independent circulation of Acts. Its companion volume had other associates, Gospels very much like itself in character and scope. Classification by contents or subject matter rather than by author is good library practice today, and it was natural that the Gospel of Luke should be associated with other Gospels both before and after the possibility arose of closer physical association of books of such size. For that possibility did arise from the introduction of an entirely different form of book, the leaf book or codex.

The exact story of this interesting alternative in book making is not known. In Christian circles at least it began much earlier than was formerly supposed, perhaps early in the second century.[9] The roll and the codex coexisted side by side for some time, but the codex had obvious advantages where a work was long, or where it was desirable to bring separate works of substantial length together.

K

The importance of the adoption of a codex format in connection with the history of the canon has never been fully appreciated.[10] This is because up to recently it was supposed that the making of the canon preceded the change. Now that the two are known to be nearly contemporary it is worth while to notice their possible relation. It has always been supposed that the canon came into being by combinations. Perhaps this was more important than selection. One early combination was the four Gospels, whether as four books each complete, or interwoven as in the *Diatessaron* of Tatian. Of course they could still be copied on several scrolls. No one will deny that the establishment of the idea of a four-fold Gospel would be much easier if all four books could be bound together in a codex than if one merely had a mental list of four separate scrolls. The Greek parchment fragment of the *Diatessaron* found at Dura-Europos belongs to the early third century and is apparently from a roll.[11] But sooner or later the codex facilitated publication of the continuous text of the whole gospel unit. Our four Gospels apparently quite early were sub-divisions of a larger unit which bore the title in the singular 'Gospel' with sub-headings 'According to Matthew', 'According to Mark', etc. This is the evidence of the earliest codices. This policy tended to divorce Acts from its companion Gospel.

The other early combination behind our New Testament is the letters of Paul. Obviously they also first existed separately. There is reason to believe that even more often and earlier than the Gospels were letters of Paul combined in a single fixed order.[12] The fact that the Gospels so long appeared in various orders in the manuscripts or lists in which all four occur suggests that the tendency to combine them was much later. There is evidence by the middle of the second century that Paul's letters had been brought together. One author, writing at about that time what we call Second Peter, speaks of letters of Paul in the plural with the word 'all' (3 : 15, 16). Marcion, the heretic, whom we usually place at Rome and at about A.D. 140, apparently had a collection of ten letters, which, except for deviations in content and in one case of name, were the same ten which are found in our New Testaments under Paul's name, though we have three more, those to Timothy and Titus.

This collection of Paul's letters also has some bearing on our thought about the history of Acts. On the one hand it has been proposed, especially by Professor E. J. Goodspeed and his pupils,[13] that the publication of Acts gave occasion to this collection. It called attention to the figure of Paul, and some unknown reader of Acts was led thereby to a further literary enterprise. This was not merely the search for letters of Paul, but, as the theory goes, he collected and 'published' them, arranging them in a given order and adding, probably prefixing, a summary of his own, embodying the ideas and to a large extent the phraseology of the original letters, especially of Colossians. This prefatory summary is what we now call Ephesians.

Though this attractive theory was devised mainly to account for the puzzling phenomena of Ephesians, it recognizes that at some time the letters of Paul must have been collected, and it suggests that this was due to the influence of Acts. For that reason mention of it is appropriate here. Probably without this stimulus a desire for such a collection would have arisen in someone else's mind at some other time. We may doubt whether at a later time so many of the genuine remains of Paul could have been found and assembled. As it is, some of his writings have certainly been lost. But the collecting of what we have was in itself an important event, and, if due to the writing of Acts, no less to be emphasized because for the collecting of Paul's letters as well as for the writing of Acts itself the time and place and person must be largely conjectures. I may perhaps add that for the Pauline corpus the conjectures have been forthcoming in the twentieth century as for the writing of the Book of Acts in the second century. Of Acts I shall be speaking later. For the Pauline corpus they are: the place, Ephesus; the time, about A.D. 90; the author, Onesimus, once the runaway slave of Philemon of Colossae, and later the bishop of Ephesus.[14]

Some scholars have reversed the relation and believe that the author of Acts knew some of our letters of Paul.[15] This view prevailed at one time, just as the other assumption prevails now.

In any case if he knew the letters he made limited use of them. Most of the passages in Luke-Acts where Enslin and others find influence of Paul's letters are where the author is writing independently of his itinerary source for Paul, viz. in the earlier parts of Paul's life (Acts 7-12) or in speeches, including Luke 22 : 19b, 20 and 24 : 34. That he should not try to fit the data of Paul's letters into the itinerary will be understood by modern scholars who have tried to do so and such a course agrees with his apparent practice in the Gospel of using his sources in segregated blocks, rather than intermingling them.

Whether or not the Book of Acts and the Pauline corpus had in origin any connection the connection between them later was inevitable. They stood to each other as do the respective biographical sources of what we often call the life and letters. Indeed the Book of Acts occupies a strategic position in the history of the canon.

For, as already suggested, the canon apparently began with two partial collections. The Gospel was one of them, the Apostle Paul was the other. The oldest known canon is that of Marcion, and it already joins the two elements. It was different from the orthodox canon in that its Gospel was only one of the four Gospels, the Gospel of Luke, and that in a somewhat different form, and that its Apostle included only ten letters of Paul in somewhat different form also. Whether because of Marcion or independently, other Christians came to combine similar two ingredients into a New Testament.

But the ingredients were not inherently connected or of similar authority. They needed something to bring them together. Passing and rather fanciful connections could be suggested, as that the Gospel of Luke was the gospel preached by Paul and its author the brother whose praise is in the gospel (2 Cor. 8 : 18), and that Paul was the disciple that Jesus loved (John 13 : 23; Gal. 2 : 20). But a better connection was needed. The gospel ingredient had undoubtedly the greater authority. Just as for the earliest Christians the authorities were the Old Testament and Jesus, so in the next stage they were the Old Testament and the Gospel. This situation is echoed in sundry early Christian passages. No other Christian writings ever received the prestige or the circulation of the Gospels or gospel corpus. Of course, in time, just as the Apostles came to have a place of authority next to Jesus, so their writings came to apply for recognition next to the Gospels. Here the first and most substantial and most well established applicant was the body of Paul's letters. They were already widely read aloud in the churches as were the Gospels. But what credentials had Paul? He was not one of the Twelve. He claimed equal authority with them, but it would be better if a vindication not his own could be quoted. Harnack[16] suggests that the Book of Acts supplied the credentials. As Christ had appointed the Twelve, so they in turn recognized Paul as an Apostle. The evidence of this is in the Book of Acts, and by including Paul as an Apostle and making him parallel with Peter, this book could be understood to be representative of the whole group of Apostles, who in turn stood for Christ and carried out his commission. They continued what Jesus 'began both to do and to teach' as this record tells us.

Thus in several ways the Book of Acts provided the keystone joining the two earlier collections. While it bore witness to the apostles it was companion volume to a Gospel. The identity of authorship when the two books were separated either was never forgotten or was inevitably rediscovered and newly recognized. Acts had close links with the Paul of the Epistles as it had with the Jesus of Luke's Gospel. And it suggested the whole apostolic mission and authority of which Paul was only one. No book was more representative of the larger apostolic circle.

But as the Book of Acts represents figuratively the arch, lintel or keystone between the two old columns of the canon, so literally its connection is neither with the one nor with the other exclusively. It was never restored to its primitive place as the continuation of Luke. The modern scholars' phrase 'Luke-Acts' was invented only recently. It is true that, when the codex permitted physical association, Acts sometimes was bound in with the four Gospels. That is the case of the early Chester Beatty Papyrus,[17] it is true of the later but famous Codex Bezae, but evidently over sixty pages once intervened in it between Gospels and Acts. Nowhere so far as I know when these five books were copied, with or without others in the New Testament, were they arranged in such a way that Luke immediately preceded Acts. Luke occurs last in neither the usual order of Gospels nor in the 'Western' order, that is Matthew, John, Luke, Mark. The so-called Cheltenham Canon[18] has the unique order Matthew, Mark, John, Luke; but here the Pauline Epistles precede the Acts of the Apostles. In the end Acts came to be associated in manuscripts neither with the Gospels nor with Paul but with the Catholic Epistles. Perhaps this was due to considerations of balanced size of the several units, but it coincided with the view that Acts belonged not with Paul alone or with any one apostle, but with such a variety of Apostles as was expressed by the names of these associated epistles,—Peter, James, Jude and John. In many lists however as in our current Bibles, Acts is found between the four Gospels and the letters of Paul. Its strategic relation to both is thus perhaps unintentionally suggested by its middle position.

Another event in the history of Acts was its acquisition of a name. The need of a name for each volume was a further result of the separation of Acts from the Gospel. The original work, if it had a name at all, can hardly have been named by the terms now applied to its separate parts. The naming of Acts was under different conditions from those surrounding other New Testament books. The four Gospels, or rather, as they appear to have been called, the Gospel, constituted a single work in four parts. Those parts needed names to distinguish them. Such distinction rather then authorship is suggested by the preposition adopted, 'according to.' Thus we have not only the terms 'according to Matthew', 'according to Luke', etc., but also, for the uncanonical gospels, 'according to the Hebrews', 'according to the Egyptians.' If another apocryphal work was not called the Gospel of Peter but according to Peter, that was in spite of the fact that unlike any of the other Gospels it never seemed anonymous but professed in its text to be written by Peter.

Of course the same is true of the New Testament Epistles and Apocalypse. With few exceptions these all in their first sentence, mostly in their first word, indicate the writer. The phrases 'of

Paul', 'of Peter', 'of James', etc., appear naturally in their titles. Where Paul's letters indicate the church or person addressed, that name is included also in the title. Where letters are unique in respect neither of author nor addressee, they are arranged according to length and distinguished by number, as in two to Corinth, Thessalonica or Timothy, or two of Peter and three of John. But the Book of Acts is in a different category. It could have been called the second narrative to Theophilus, but its companion had acquired a different classification. Just how its present title came to be we no longer know. In fact its title varies in the oldest references or manuscripts between Acts and Acts of the Apostles. The Greek word for 'Acts' is not unique among titles of historical works. It represents in one case the Latin 'res gestae'. The noteworthy thing about the title of Acts among our New Testament titles is the absence of a personal name following, either in the form of a simple genitive or as with the Gospels in the formula 'according to'. Though at some times much stress was laid upon the author of Acts as an accredited person suitable for a scripture writer, 'this is not brought out in the title which was given to the book . . . Reflection upon the content of the book was the more important element in the composition of the title.'[19] 'To the Hebrews' alone of the New Testament books presented in its early title a like degree of anonymity. The two volumes Luke and Acts, if first discovered and named by modern scholars, would probably have been given a single name and one like the anonymous Epistle to Diognetus or the four books of rhetoric *Ad Herennium* traditionally assigned to Cornificius. They are *Ad Theophilum*, Books I and II.

Whether such anonymity prevailed among the readers of Luke and Acts for any considerable time we do not know. The books are not quoted much in the surviving literature. The first person of whom the ancients affirmed knowledge of either of these books is Marcion. He lived apparently A.D. 140. His critics said that he published a form of the Gospel of Luke but did not indicate for it any author. I do not think he knew the Book of Acts, at least I believe we have no evidence that he did.[20] For our present purpose orthodoxy and heresy do not concern us, but we must recognize that these considerations had influence in the thought and debate of the time. In controversy with Marcion over the Gospel of Luke Tertullian vigorously maintained the impropriety of using a book without clear identification of authorship.

But the authorship of these two books was so obviously one and the same man, that their situation in this regard could not well be separated for one who knew both volumes. If Marcion did not know the authorship of Luke he did not know that of Acts either. If others affirmed the authorship of either volume they could only assign the same origin to the other volume.

We have evidence beginning not long after the time of Marcion that Christians assigned one or both volumes to Luke. It is found in the Canon of Muratori, in Irenaeus, in Clement of Alexandria, in Tertullian, to go no further than the half century from about 175 to 225. Since these four writers represent Rome, Gaul, Alexandria and North Africa the view was already widespread. It may have been already current when in distinguishing the collected Gospels one was called according to Luke. Justin Martyr seems to have known our Gospel of Luke, and it is therefore one of the Gospels or memorabilia which he describes as written by the Apostles and those that followed them. This emphasis upon followers of Apostles as well as on Apostles themselves is explicit in the later discussions of Mark and Luke.

For quite apart from controversy and the question of name there is evidence that Christians like the four writers here mentioned were interested in the origin of the two books to Theophilus. They read them to find out what the books themselves said or disclosed about the author's procedure and accomplishment. Let me cite one writer fully. The Canon of Muratori[21] says that he wrote the Gospel after the ascension of Christ when Paul had taken him as companion on his journey. He wrote on the basis of report. He had not seen the Lord in the flesh and therefore as he could trace the course of events he set them down. So also he began the story with the birth of John. . . . But the Acts of all the Apostles were written in one volume. He compiled for most excellent Theophilus what things were done in detail in his presence, as he plainly shows by omitting both the death of Peter and also the departure of Paul from the city [of Rome], when he departed for Spain.[22]

I need hardly point out how easily all this can be deduced from no more knowledge than reading Luke-Acts. This work begins with the birth of John, and ends without telling either of the death of Peter or of the anticipated departure of Paul from Rome to Spain. The Christians believed on the basis of plans or predictions in other books that both these events took place but they did not find them in Acts. Why? What they did find at the end of Acts were narratives in the first person plural. That pronoun was naturally assumed to imply the author's presence at events thus narrated. He was in fact a companion of Paul. Therefore he may be assumed not to have been present at events not narrated. Just as he was not present at events that might have been included in Acts and so omitted them so he was not an eyewitness to the events in the Third Gospel. There he wrote on the basis of report. At this point one recognizes the manifold influence of the preface of the Gospel. For there the author plainly distinguishes himself and his fellows (another 'us') from the eyewitnesses, who had reported the events, yet he had traced the course of events. He was writing in detail (or accurately). He addressed his work to most excellent Theophilus.

The later writer uses all these statements when he declares that the evangelist had written most excellently (perhaps by a confusion of the adverbial and vocative endings in Latin) to Theophilus. He had not seen the Lord in the flesh and yet he wrote in his own name rather than in that of his informants. He had traced the course of all the events. This last phrase from the preface could alternatively have been understood as meaning he had followed all of the eyewitnesses and ministers. This masculine 'all' may be echoed in the phrase 'Acts of all the apostles' in the Canon of Muratori, and in the frequent reference to this or other gospel writers as being followers of the apostles which we find in the later authors Irenaeus and Tertullian and perhaps also earlier in Justin and Papias.[23] The latter two being extant in

Greek show that they are using the same verb for 'follow' as in Luke's preface.

In fact the lore current in the late second and early third century about the origin of Acts is apparently much of it due to the thoughtful and imaginative deduction from some of the passages in Luke-Acts. What I have quoted from the Canon of Muratori can be so explained and I have quoted everything except 'Luke', and 'Luke that physician'. One cannot therefore but wonder whether, even the author's name was similarly deduced. The identity of this writer, who was a follower of Paul but not originally of Jesus, would constitute a basis for curiosity and conjecture. The author of Acts accompanies Paul to Rome, and it was while in prison at Rome that Paul seemed to later Christians to have written Second Timothy and other prison letters. What more natural than to supplement the material provided by Luke-Acts about its author by reference to what the Epistles say of Paul's associates at Rome? In Colossians and Philemon those who send greetings are three Jews, Aristarchus, Mark, Jesus Justus, and three Gentiles, Epaphras, Luke and Demas. Now Aristarchus and Mark would seem to ancient readers of Acts excluded because they are mentioned in that book by name. Of the others a decisive but uncritical clue may well have been found in the passage in Second Timothy 4 where the absence of Demas, Mark and others is noted in contrast to the simple statement 'Only Luke is with me'. This Luke had been further characterized in Colossians as 'the beloved physician'. If one assumed today that the 'we' of Acts includes the author and that the latter was present at Rome throughout the two year imprisonment there, and that this Roman imprisonment was the one implied in Paul's Epistles, nobody could probably make any better conjecture. The ancient church provided no alternative conjecture. There was no reason why it should, and it preferred to accept this solution rather than leave the authorship undetermined.

In contrast to the unity of opinion about the author of Acts among Christian readers near the end of the second century stands a striking lack of unity at that time in the matter of the wording of its text. Like all books copied by hand Acts was subject to vicissitudes due to accidental errors and more conscious changes made by its copyists. But more than in any other early Christian book known to us this book displays a variation so constant or frequent that one can only think of the book as circulating in two forms of text. Both forms are early, both have a certain consistency of character, so that their general relation can be described; each has its own history and area of distribution. In spite of the misleading character of their traditional names I shall continue to call them the Neutral text and the Western text respectively. Simpler and less question begging would be the terms shorter and longer. Each text sometimes has not what the other contains but the Western text is in general longer than the Neutral.[24] Many of its additions are the expansion or multiplication of religious phrases like Jesus the Lord, the Lord Jesus Christ, and Jesus Christ, in each case for the single word Jesus. It often inserts the adverb 'then'. But more often the difference is between a more diffuse and circumstantial account and a terser more condensed narrative. I take almost at random the account of the vision at Troas (16: 9-10) In the familiar text it reads:

> And a vision appeared to Paul at night: a man of Macedonia was standing beseeching him and saying, 'Come over to Macedonia and help us.' And when he had seen the vision, immediately we sought to go on into Macedonia, concluding that God had called us to preach the gospel to them. Setting sail therefore from Troas, etc.

The Western text reads as follows:

> And in a vision at night there appeared to Paul as it were a man of Macedonia standing before him beseeching and saying, 'Come over to Macedonia and help us.' When, therefore, he awoke he related the vision to us, and we perceived that the Lord had called us to preach the gospel to those in Macedonia. On the morrow setting sail from Troas, etc.

The total number of words in these passages is nearly the same, but the slight rearrangement of clauses, the additions, the exchange of synonyms are characteristic of the differences in parallels throughout the Book of Acts. Many of the additions in the longer text could be taken for granted in the shorter, such as the phrase that the man was standing 'before' Paul, that Paul related the vision, and on the other side the statement in one version that immediately we sought to go into Macedonia is paralleled only by the addition of the phrase 'on the morrow' in the following sentence of the other version.

Here are two forms of the story of the sons of Sceva (19: 13-15):

> And some of the itinerant Jewish exorcists undertook to pronounce the name of the Lord Jesus over those who had evil spirits, saying, 'I adjure you by the Jesus whom Paul preaches.' And there were seven sons of a certain Sceva, a Jewish high priest, doing this. But the evil spirit answered them, 'Jesus I know and Paul I know; but who are you?'

> And some of the itinerant Jewish exorcists undertook to pronounce the name of the Lord Jesus over those who had evil spirits, saying 'I adjure you by the Jesus whom Paul preaches.' Among whom also sons of Sceva, a certain priest, wished to do the same thing (they had a custom of exorcizing such persons), and coming in to the possessed man they began to call upon the name, saying, 'By Jesus whom Paul preaches we command you to come out.' Then the evil spirit answered, saying, 'Jesus I know and Paul I know; but who are you?'

More famous and familiar is the variation, partly repeated in the three accounts of the apostolic decree, given at the close of a letter cited (15: 28-29):

> For it has seemed good to the Holy Spirit and to us to lay upon you no greater burden than these necessary things: that you abstain from what has been sacrificed to idols and from blood and from what is strangled and from unchastity. In guarding yourselves from these, you will do well. Farewell.

> For it has seemed good to the Holy Spirit and to us to lay upon you no greater burden than these necessary things: that you abstain from what has been sacrificed to idols and from blood and

from unchastity and that you do not do to another what you do not wish to have done to you. In guarding yourselves from these, you did well, being sustained by the Holy Spirit. Farewell.

Yet in between such variant short passages the Neutral and Western texts are often almost completely identical.

The existence of two texts in Acts so similar as to be not independent, so different as not to be merely the accumulation of usual variants in copying, has posed to scholars a difficult if not insoluble problem. How did two such texts arise? If they are due to paraphrase, which is the paraphrase of the other? Which on grounds of vivid and accurate detail is to be accounted the earlier? And what does our knowledge of the times and places where each form of text can be found suggest as a solution?

This problem has claimed attention of many scholars over many years. The solutions suggested have been very varied. I do not intend to review them fully here. One of the simplest and most attractive is the view that the original author issued the Book of Acts in two forms.[25] That cuts the Gordian knot very easily. It is like the famous phrase of the Dodo in *Alice in Wonderland* that 'everybody has won, and all must have prizes.' Both accounts according to this view are equally authentic, and while the question remains which version is the earlier and why was the earlier one rewritten, if they come from the same author the difference in age and in historic value cannot be very important.

There are some considerations which make this solution more probable than at first appears. Neither of the versions of Acts is without the distinctive style of this author. Where the Western text has additions they often use the vocabulary of the common material. For the original author such consistency would be natural. An alien reviser might be expected to betray himself by an alien style.[26] But why do the facts and meaning of the two texts when parallel sometimes differ? The original author shows in the undisputed text of his work a freedom of paraphrase. The differences between the two accounts of Jesus and his disciples at the end of Luke and the beginning of Acts, between the two accounts of the conversion of Cornelius, or the three accounts of the conversion of Paul are not unlike the kind of differences in expression or even in detail that exist between the Western and the Neutral text of Acts.

Another view is that the Western text of Acts arose as follows: The primitive Greek text of our four Gospels and Acts came into the hands of a Jewish Christian who freely turned it into Aramaic. The treatment shows the Jewish Christian slant, Palestinian local colour, the influence of the Hebrew Old Testament, and a certain freedom of rewriting or expansion which is not inaptly called 'targumic'. This Aramaic was then translated back into Greek, somewhat literally as regards its Semitic idiom. But the new translator had the earlier Greek before him and frequently could follow it word for word and still render his Aramaic original literally. At other times he shows his independence by choosing synonyms of the earlier Greek. Where his Aramaic source was different in substance from the Greek, his Greek translation follows the Aramaic often somewhat literally. Although this process took place not long after the beginning of the second century so that the Western text circulated as early as and more widely than its rival, it is worthless for the reconstruction of the prior Greek. This explanation of the phenomena I need hardly add is the invention of Professor C. C. Torrey.[27] It is ingenious and it accounts for at least some of the facts. Its appeal to us will depend on how far we accept his more general view of the currency of Aramaic Christian literature in the first and second century. But it does not require our acceptance of his other theory that our standard text of the Gospels and of the first half of Acts was also translated from Aramaic.

A third view of the relation of the two forms of text is connected with the name of A. C. Clark. In his later study of Acts[28] he adopted the view that the Western text was original, and that the Neutral text is due to an abbreviator. He emphasized the liveliness, vividness and apparent factual veracity of some of the longer readings, and he believed that they were not expansions such as are characteristic of scribes, but details which have been lost at the hands of the man who paraphrased it into our shorter standard Greek. He thought the longer text was before this man in cola, with one phrase to the line, and that the abbreviator simply left out many whole lines.

The fourth view, most fully and circumstantially presented by Professor Ropes,[29] is just the opposite. On the whole the shorter text seems to him original and the additions to it rarely of any value. He does not deny that among the additions may be preserved a few quite early and authentic data,[30] and that the shorter text may sometimes include quite primitive error. While the reasons for creating the Western text are not quite evident, it was, he believes, definitely the work of an individual paraphraser and not merely an indiscriminate congeries of erratic readings from every quarter.

These rival views of the problem are not easily appreciated without a great deal of additional information. Nothing takes the place of reading side by side the two versions of the Book of Acts, noticing the most minute detail and considering the possible motives behind both variants wherever the texts differ.[30a] The matter is complicated by the fact that the phenomena in Acts appear, though in a less degree, in Luke, and to some extent in the other Gospels also. The textual sources line up against each other in much the same companies. A solution of the problem in Acts must take cognizance of the parallel though partly opposite data in these other books. All the solutions discussed postulate a definite, somewhat homogeneous process taking place at a given time and producing thereby two editions of Acts rather than one.

We may not know just when or how this situation began. Professor Ropes thought possibly the drastic rewriting which we call the Western text was done in the same circle in which the collecting of the books into what we now call the canon of the New Testament was taking place.[31] My feeling is that the latter process was largely unconscious. It is possible, however, in tracing the history of Acts at least to recognize that there were these two forms of text, that both have claim to great age and one of them to wide circulation. It has been stated that 'at the end of the second century no region of the Christian world was unacquainted with the "Western" text of Acts'.[32] The Neutral text is found early primarily in Egypt and Alexandria, but there is no reason to suppose it later became less widespread. The better or older product has not always the widest currency.

This matter of text is only one of several problems about Acts of which it may be said that none of the proposed solutions is entirely satisfactory. Often, if one must choose, the choice can be justified as nothing better than the least unsatisfactory of alternatives. One has the unhappy feeling that other possibilities exist so unexpected that only a knowledge of the actual facts would recover them. Sometimes when we do know the causes of literary phenomena we realize that without that knowledge no one would guess the real history of the document in question. As has been said of the problem here before us: 'There must be a human explanation of these discrepancies, but our present knowledge does not suffice to provide it. All that we can do is to consider each successive explanation as it is offered, and to test it in the light of bibliographical knowledge, of human probabilities, and of common sense.'[33]

The textual situation leaves one uneasy. Some of the phrases in Acts selected for mention in earlier chapters are not to be stressed. One recalls that even the shorter Neutral text has clauses not supported by the Western. If the Western is even in these few cases correct we shall have been quoting inferior readings. Thus we must recall that the phrase 'no mean city' (21 : 39) is not in the Western text, nor the word 'poets' in the expression 'some of your own poets have said' (17 : 28).[34] In the account of the Council at Jerusalem the omission of 'things strangled' and the addition of the Golden Rule (15 : 20, 29 and, without the Golden Rule, 21 : 25) transform the decision from ritual or ceremonial regulations to moral ones.[35] The reference in 27 : 1 to the Augustan cohort may have been missing too.

Since I have mentioned personal names in my previous chapters I may call attention to some variations in our texts in that regard.

	Neutral	Western
1 : 23	Joseph Barsabbas	Joseph Barnabas[36]
4 : 6	John	Jonathan
13 : 6	Barjesus	Barjesua
13 : 8	Elymas	Etoemas
15 : 22	Judas Barsabbas	Judas Barabbas
18 : 7	Titius Justus	Justus
18 : 24	Apollos	Apollonius
19 : 9	Tyrannus	Tyrannius
20 : 4	Tychicus	Eutychus
21 : 16	Mnason	Nason

I have already mentioned the attractive Western reading in 20:4 which corrects the epithet for Gaius the Macedonian (19:29) from 'of Derbe' to 'of Douberus'. There is a curious difference in the treatment of Priscilla and Aquila in chapter 18. The Neutral text never mentions Aquila without Priscilla and except at the first introduction always puts the woman first. The Western text departs from it in both respects.[37]

Among other matters where the Western text and the Neutral differ are some affecting the inner clues of authorship. The exact limits of the 'we' passages are not quite identical. The pronoun comes in or goes out a sentence earlier or later in the various texts or manuscripts.[38] This is true of the familiar four passages beginning with the vision at Troas quoted earlier. More striking is the instance occuring five chapters before and referring to several years earlier (11 : 28) where, in reporting a visit to Antioch of Paul, the Western text includes the inconspicuous subordinate clause 'when we were gathered together'. It is possible that this 'we' is due to the appearance in a later list of prophets and teachers at Antioch (13 : 1) of one Lucius of Cyrene. Now Lucius is one of the common Roman names and Luke (Latin, Lucas) is an alternate form of it. Is this reading due to a feeling that the first person implied in the 'we' should be used if Lucius is identical with Luke of Paul's letters and if that is identical with the Lucius of Acts? Indeed one old text of the list of Antioch reads not merely 'Lucius of Cyrene' but 'Lucas of

Cyrene' and another 'Lucius of Cyrene who remains until now'. Like some of the five hundred brethren to whom the vision of Christ appeared (1 Cor. 15 : 6), he had not died but at the time of writing was still alive. If he was believed to be the author of Acts this change is natural. A more definite variant to the same effect occurs in some Syriac sources for the text at Acts 20 : 13 where in place of 'we' (here excluding Paul) was read 'I, Luke, and those with me'. If the attribution of Lucan authorship to Acts rests on the knowledge of the letters of Paul, then these readings cannot belong to an author of Acts ignorant of Paul's letters. There are one or two other places where the Western text can be understood as harmonizing with the Epistles.

We have suggested already that the Book of Acts helped in the canonization of the letters of Paul. It probably helped also in defining the authority of Luke's Gospel among the Gospels. The common authorship of the two books was accepted and the 'we' in parts of Acts was understood to include the 'me' in the Gospel preface (1 : 3) and to identify him as a companion of Paul's travels. What about the canonical authority of Acts itself? It followed in time but not necessarily at once. The prestige which it gave to others may have lagged for itself. There is no reason to suppose that Marcion rejected it, in the sense that others already had it in a kind of canon and that he deliberately omitted it. We do not know that there was any orthodox canon so early as his time. His critics of the next generation and of ours, assuming the later canon, probably do him an injustice. Selection does not imply rejection of what others have not yet selected. Neither Irenaeus nor Tertullian indicates that Marcion knew the Book of Acts to reject it or accept it.[39]

Well before Tertullian's time Acts was generally included in the New Testament canon. That in itself insured some circulation and acquaintance, but we should like to know something more of its use both before and after this time. For the former period that is impossible. As Harnack notes, 'We have no knowledge, or as good as no knowledge, of the Acts before it makes its appearance in the New Testament.'[40] The best known books were undoubtedly those publicly read in Christian gatherings. These were the prophets and the 'memorabilia' of the Apostles as Justin Martyr names them a dozen times. The former may mean Old Testament scriptures, which were certainly read in Christian assemblies, the latter are defined by Justin elsewhere as 'called gospels'. The term does not therefore mean memorabilia about the apostles nor does it refer to the Book of Acts.[41] Justin's genuine works, though somewhat extensive, have, I believe, no clear evidence of knowledge of that writing. Even his reference to Simon Magus, a fellow Samaritan of his from the town of Gittae who in the reign of Claudius came to Rome like Justin himself later and received divine honours, has no mark of knowledge of the reference to Simon in the Book of Acts. Justin uses the word apostles in connection with the Gospels as we have noted and a dozen other times, but the individuals and events that he mentions in connection with the word, except Christ the apostle of God and John of the Book of Revelation, could be derived from the Gospels, from the general tradition and from the Old Testament.[42] They are not from Acts.

The same negative situation is true of the other apologists and of the generally earlier writings which go under the name of the Apostolic Fathers. Supposed echoes in them reminiscent of the Book of Acts are usually just such language as is found in the Old Testament or in independent Greek writing. Those parts of the Pastoral Epistles which have been regarded as not genuine and therefore later than Paul and Acts show no knowledge of the latter volume.[43]

Less familiar to most of us are the apocryphal Acts of the Apostles. Those of Peter, of Paul and of John are the earliest in date probably. Contrary to the natural assumption, they are not written in imitation of the canonical Acts, nor do their narratives coincide with or continue the episodes in Acts. Their names of persons are more likely derived from the Epistles. Their motifs are as much characteristic of the Old Testament, of the Gospels and of contemporary Greek writings as of the second volume to Theophilus.[44] Even the word 'acts' when used of them is not necessarily borrowed, since the canonical book's title with the

plural of apostles, or even more of 'all the apostles' may be independent or due to the uncanonical works rather than vice versa.

Knowledge of our Book of Acts is evidenced to us first to-
wards the end of the second century and by the same writers to
whom it is already scripture. From then on it shares the history
of the central nucleus of the canon. Like the Gospels and the
epistles it was early translated into both Syriac and Latin. Not all
books were translated necessarily at the same time exactly, but
there is a likeness in character and probably in date between the
Old Latin as it is called of the Gospels and of Acts, and so with
the Old Syriac though the latter in the case of Acts is even more
imperfectly known to us.

At this point our story emerges into more light. The completely unrecorded history of Acts is over. Irenaeus quotes substantial passages and discusses the book; so do Tertullian, Origen
and later writers. A single quotation may show clear knowledge
of the book. Thus in a letter from the churches of Vienne and
Lyons in Gaul comparable in date and place with Irenaeus we
read that the martyrs 'prayed for those who had inflicted cruel-
ties upon them, even as Stephen the perfect witness, "Lord, lay
not this sin to their charge".'[45] Clement of Alexandria compares
another passage when he writes ' . . . just as Luke in the Acts of
the Apostles records Paul as saying: "Men of Athens, I perceive
that in all things ye are too superstitious"', etc.[46]

The canonization of Acts was, as we have suggested, not so
early as that of the Gospels, and even when it was used as canonical or as establishing the canonicity of other writings we have
hints of its own inferior position. For Clement of Alexandria and
I think also for Irenaeus only the Gospels stood on a par with the
Old Testament. For Clement and for others Acts was associated
quite freely with books of deuterocanonical or uncanonical
rank. Clement cites alongside of Acts the Leucian Acts of John,
the traditions of Matthias and especially the Preaching of Peter.
In Codex Claromontanus our book is listed at the close of the
New Testament and in doubtful company. The list ends:
Epistle of Barnabas, Revelation of John, Acts of the Apostles,
Hermas, Acts of Paul, Revelation of Peter.[47] Only at long last

was the line drawn which once for all put our Acts of the Apostles inside a closed canon of Scripture.

But as we know quite well today circulation of canonized writings does not prove equal familiarity of all books or parts of books. The early Christian knowledge of Acts tended to be selective. What was usable in controversy might not be most edifying in preaching. Those who were interested in theology might have little interest in narrative. To some early Christians (and later ones too) the speeches were the most interesting. Jerome about A.D. 400 writes that to many in his time the Book of Acts was of no interest because it seemed to sound forth naked history,[48] and Chrysostom, his contemporary, who in exactly that year writes the first extant treatise on Acts, begins his first homily by saying that at his time 'to many persons this book is so little known, both it and its author, that they are not even aware that there is such a book in existence'.[49] In an earlier homily he referred to the matter in Acts as 'a strange new dish . . . strange, I say and not strange. Not strange, for it belongs to the order of Holy Scripture; and yet strange, because peradventure your ears are not accustomed to such a subject. Certainly there are many to whom this book is not even known, and many again think it so plain that they slight it. Thus to some men their ignorance, to others their knowledge is the cause of the neglect'.[50]

By these quotations from the end of the fourth century I may seem to have skipped over without mention a substantial interval in the history of the Book of Acts. As a matter of fact few sustained discussions of the Book, either in the way of homilies, like Chrysostom's or in commentaries or scholia, have come down to us. Ephrem the Syrian who died in 373 wrote a commentary on Acts in Syriac. It is brief and cursory but with special emphasis on the speeches in Acts. This is preserved to us in an Armenian translation and also embedded in an Armenian catena on Acts, the latter largely based on Chrysostom. The printed Greek catena on Acts is also more than half from Chrysostom. Apparently Ammonius of Alexandria and Didymus the Blind are the only other fourth or fifth century Greek

Fathers quoted in these catenas as writers of continuous exposition of Acts.

A papyrus booklet of the same century (P 50) gives us one interesting illustration of how Acts could be excerpted for a given purpose. It contains on its four pages first Acts 8 : 26-32, then 10: 26-31. 'Neither records in its entirety the narrative from which it is taken. Rather they comprise just enough of the stories of Philip and the Ethiopian eunuch, and of Peter and Cornelius, to show how two Christian Apostles acting under divine instruction came to disregard the barriers upon them by the law and "attached themselves" to pagans. Κολλᾶσθαι is actually the one important word that appears in both selections. This being so it is not unreasonable to suggest that P 50 was written in service of missionary or homiletic purposes or both.'[51]

In the centuries that followed Chrysostom selective interest in the book, ignorance of it or neglect have probably often been the pattern. It has been pointed out that we have only seven complete uncial manuscripts of Acts.[52] The limited references to it would be interesting to follow through the years. Like the book itself for its own time they would reflect contemporary colour. There is reason to think that often the speeches received the most attention. A mere leafing through Ropes' edition of the text shows that Irenaeus quotes in extenso the speeches of chapters 2, 3, 4, 5 (30-32), 7 (2-8, 38-43), 10, 14, 15 (including the letter), 17 and 20.[53] We note that Clement of Alexandria quotes at length the speech at Athens (17), and that the patristic evidence is particularly full for this passage. Our generation has its own preferences. We may not be so averse to 'naked history' as were Jerome's contemporaries. In that case we have been justified in considering the book's own place in history.

NOTES ON CHAPTER VI

1. Terentianus Maurus, De syllabis 1286 (Keil, Gramm. Lat. vi, p. 363).
2. The Making of Luke-Acts, New York, The Macmillan Co., 1927.
3. Cf. ibid., pp. 352-360.
4. See Beginnings of Christianity, iv, 349.
5. To the question asked by de Zwaan, Was the Book of Acts a Posthum-

ous Edition? (*Harvard Theological Review*, 17, 1924, pp. 95 ff.), Harnack, *The Acts of the Apostles*, Eng. Trans., 1909, p. 48, also gives an affirmative answer.

6. For the meaning, in this connection, of the address to Theophilus see *Making of Luke-Acts*, pp. 201-204, and A. D. Nock, *Gnomon*, 25, 1953, p. 501 (an important study of Acts in the modest form of a review of Dibelius). The older authority on all matters of the sort was Theodor Birt. On publication and dedication see his *Abriss des antiken Buchwesens* (Iwan von Müller, *Handbuch der klassischen Altertumswissenschaft*, I, iii), 1913, pp. 307-315. This work corrects and supplements his better known *Das antike Buchwesen*, 1882, and *Die Buchrolle*, 1907.

7. F. G. Kenyon, *Handbook to the Textual Criticism of the New Testament*, 2nd edit., 1926, p. 34.

8. H. St. J. Thackeray, *The Septuagint and Jewish Worship*, 1921, Appendix IV.

9. F. G. Kenyon, *The Western Text in the Gospels and Acts*, (Proceedings of the British Academy 1938, vol. 24, pp. 287-315), 1938, p. 20. See also H. A. Sanders, 'Beginnings of the Modern Book,' in *Michigan Alumnus Quarterly Review*, xliv, 1938, pp. 95 ff., and C. H. Roberts, The Christian Book and the Greek Papyri, *The Journal of Theological Studies*, 50, 1949, pp. 155-168, cf. *ibid.*, 40, 1939, pp. 253-257. Both Roberts, p. 160 f., and McCown (see next note) think many New Testament books but not Luke or Acts were from the beginning written in codex form.

10. See however C. C. McCown, Codex and Roll in the New Testament, *Harvard Theological Review*, 34, 1941, pp. 219 ff., especially 243-249.

11. C. H. Kraeling, *A Greek Fragment of Tatian's Diatessaron from Dura* (Studies and Documents III), 1935, p. 4.

12. Cf. Roberts, *Journal of Theological Studies* 50, 1949, p. 164.

13. *New Solutions of New Testament Problems*, 1927, chapters i and ii. *The Meaning of Ephesians*, 1933. Compare a new English advocate, C. Leslie Mitton, *The Epistle to the Ephesians, its Authorship, Origin and Purpose*, 1951, chapter v.

14. John Knox, *Philemon among the Letters of Paul*, 1935, 50-56. E. J. Goodspeed, *New Chapters in New Testament Study*, 1937, 31-32.

15. M. S. Enslin, 'Luke' and Paul, *Journal of the American Oriental Society*, 58, 1938, 81-91.

16. A. Harnack, *The Origin of the New Testament*, Eng. Trans., 1925, pp. 53, 64-68. The details may not be altogether certain but Harnack has shown with great probability the importance of Acts in the development of the New Testament canon. In his earlier monograph, *Das Neue Testament um das Jahr 200*, 1889, 52-54, Harnack showed how the representativeness of the Book of Acts was exaggerated to serve the purpose of those who introduced it late into the canon or who used it to establish the *twelve* apostles or *all* the apostles as of authority no less than Paul.

17. Acts originally occupied about 103 pages in this manuscript of the third century (P 45). One leaf extant of another papyrus codex of the next century (P 8) shows that Acts would fill about 56 leaves. Its page numbering indicates that Acts was the first and perhaps the only writing in the volume.

18. This is an African list of about A.D. 360. It may be conveniently con-

sulted in A. Souter, *The Text and Canon of the New Testament*, 1913, pp. 212-213 where it is printed together with more than a score of other lists. Luke is also the last gospel in the stichometry of Codex Claromontanus, perhaps of earlier date, but in this list Acts is the very last of the New Testament books (*ibid.*, pp. 211-212).

Perhaps the nearest we come to evidence that Luke and Acts were ever copied in juxtaposition is to be found in the fact that in Codex Bezae the name John (Greek Johannes) is spelled with one n regularly in these two books, but with two n's in Matthew, John and Mark. So Lippelt, as cited in E. Nestle, *Einführung in das griechische Neue Testament*, 2nd edit., 1899, p. 130. It has been suggested that this is due to the fact that in an ancestor of Codex Bezae the same scribe copied these two books and that they were in such order that Luke came just before Acts.

19. Harnack, *The Origin of the New Testament*, p. 64 note.

20. See p. 157.

21. For the unhappily defective Latin text of this second century document see Souter, *op. cit.*, pp. 208–210. The translation is accordingly uncertain in spots.

22. There is no positive statement here on the date of writing Acts. In other Christian writers one tradition is that it was written after the death of Paul, another, found first in Eusebius and based perhaps on the abrupt ending of Acts, that it was written at the point of time when the narrative in Acts ends. See A. Wikenhauser, Die altkirkliche Ueberlieferung über die Abfassungszeit der Apostelgeschichte, *Biblische Zeitschrift*, 23, 1935, pp. 365-371.

23. Luke 1:3, παρηκολουθηκότι. Papias, (Euseb., *H.E.*, iii. 39), uses the verb once of followers of the elders and once of Mark as a follower not of the Lord but of Peter; Justin Martyr. Dial. 103, 8, uses it of gospel authors as followers of the apostles. B. W. Bacon, *Revue d'Histoire et de Philosophie religieuses*, 8, 1928, pp. 209-226, understands Luke to have used the verb in this sense. For a still different understanding see H. J. Cadbury, Expositor, 8th Ser., 1922, 24, pp. 401-420.

24. J. H. Ropes, *The Beginnings of Christianity*, vol. iii, p. ccxxxii, says the Western Text is nearly one tenth longer; F. G. Kenyon, *The Western Text in the Gospels and Acts*, p. 26, says about 8½ per cent longer.

25. The most important exponents of this view in modern times have been Friedrich Blass and Theodor Zahn.

26. See F. Blass, Professor Harnack und die Schriften des Lukas (*Beiträge zur Förderung christlicher Theologie*, xi, 2), 1907.

27. *Documents of the Primitive Church*, 1941, pp. 112-148.

28. *The Acts of the Apostles*, 1933.

29. *The Beginnings of Christianity*, vol. iii., 1926.

30. 'It must never be forgotten that the basis of the "Western" revision was a text far more ancient than any MS. now extant or even any considerable patristic testimony still accessible to us.' Ropes, *op. cit.*, p. ccxxxv f.

30a. The two Greek texts may be conveniently compared in the volume of Ropes where Codex Vaticanus and Codex Bezae are printed on opposite pages. J. M. Wilson, *The Acts of the Apostles*, 1923, prints Codex Bezae in English Translation, indicating its divergences in heavy faced type.

31. Ropes, *op. cit.*, p. ccxlv.

32. Ropes, *op. cit.*, p. ccxli.

33. Kenyon, *The Western Text in the Gospels and Acts*, p. 31. M. Dibelius explained the variation as due to the fact that Acts had a double reading public—the book trade and the Christian community. The latter used it later in public lection than it used the Gospels, including Luke. Hence even the Neutral Text acquired in this book more corruptions and it needs more emendation by conjecture. *The Journal of Religion*, 21, 1941, pp. 421-431 (republished in his *Aufsätze zur Apostelgeschichte*, 1951, pp. 76-83). More recent study of the textual problem of Acts has made no clear progress. See the relevant summaries in A. F. J. Klijn, *A Survey of the Researches into the Western Text of the Gospels and Acts*, Utrecht, 1949, and J. Dupont, *Les Problems du Livre des Actes d'après les travaux recents* (Analecta Lovaniensia Biblica et Orientalia, Ser. II, fasc. 17), Louvain, 1950.

34. One wonders whether the omission of the word 'poets' in Codex Bezae and in the text used by the Latin Fathers (see *Beginnings*, iii *as loc.*) has some connexion with the habit of connecting the phrase 'some among you' with the prose words which precede it rather than with the familiar hemistich of verse which follows it. Cf. above, p. 56, note 33. Codex Bezae has further variants. It inserts the phrase 'daily' (καθ' ἡμέραν) after 'live and move and have our being', which is best accounted for as due to a gloss intended to change your to our (καθ' ἡμᾶς). See J. Rendel Harris, *Bulletin of the Bezan Club*, 8, 1930, p. 6.

35. See quotation of 15 : 28-29 above, pp. 150f.

36. For the textual evidence of each of these readings see Ropes, *ad loc.*. A confused echo of this Western variant here is found I think also in Clementine Recognitions i, 60: *Barnabas qui est Matthias*.

37. See *Beginnings*, iii on 18 : 26.

38. Ropes, *op. cit.*, p. ccxxxix.

39. That Marcion had once known Acts and later rejected it is stated apparently on the supposed authority of Tertullian by writers as separate as Richard Biscoe, *The History of the Acts*, 1742, pp. 528, 536 f., and Adolf Harnack, *Marcion*, 1921, 152* f., 2nd edit., 1924, 172* f. Cf. John Knox, *Marcion and the New Testament*, 1942, p. 121, note 7. At an earlier date Harnack wrote: 'In spite of Tertullian (*Adv. Marc.* v, 2, 3, and *De praescr.*, 22 f.) we cannot be quite certain whether the book came into the hands of Marcion; there are good reasons both for and against' (*Die Apostelgeschichte*, 1908, p. 4, note, Eng. Trans., *The Acts of the Apostles*, 1909, p. xvii, note 2). This was omitted when the essay was reprinted in his *Mission und Ausbreitung*, 4th edit., 1924, I, p. 92, note 4. Still later he writes that Marcion had rejected three Gospels, the Acts and Revelation, whereas he did not even know the Pastoral Epistles (*Die Briefsammlung des Apostels Paulus*, 1926, p. 6).

40. *The Origin of the New Testament*, p. 66, note.

41. Apol. 66 : 3. Where Tertullian uses of Acts the Latin *commentarius* which would be the equivalent to ὑπόμνημα he calls it *commentarius Lucae* (*De jejunio*, 10).

42. J. Knox, *op. cit.*, also believes that Justin as well as Marcion and Papias did not know Acts, but he cites some scholars that have believed that Justin

used Acts (p. 136, note 29). Knox further infers that Acts was not written before the time of these Fathers. That does not follow since there is as little evidence in Papias and Justin of use of the Epistles of Paul (*ibid.*, p. 115, and note).

43. This is not the view of B. S. Easton who believes that 2 Tim. 3: 11 is the first certain citation from Acts in Christian literature, although Clement 18, 1, may echo Acts 13 : 22 (*The Pastoral Epistles*, 1947). If parts of these letters are genuine, those parts like the other letters of Paul would neither be regarded as dependent on Acts nor vice versa.

44. See Rosa Söder, *Die apokryphen Apostelgeschichten und die romanhafte Literatur der Antike* (Würzburger Studien zur Altertumswissenschaft iii), 1932, p. 183 and note 3.

45. Eusebius, *H.E.* v, 2, 5. The date is usually given as A.D. 177.

46. *Strom.* v, 12, p. 696.

47. Cf. Harnack, *Das Neue Testament um das Jahr 200*, 1889, pp. 51-52. For Codex Claromontanus see above, note 18.

48. *Epist.* 53 *ad Paulinum* (Migne *P.L.* 22 : 548).

49. *Homiliae in Acta*, I.

50. *Homiliae in Principium Actorum,* iii, p. 54.

51. Papyrus 50, published by C. H. Kraeling in *Quantulacumque*, edited by R. P. Casey and others, 1937, pp. 163-172. For Ephrem's commentary see *Beginnings*, iii, pp. 373-453. On early Christians who quoted Acts see *ibid.*, pp. clxxxv-cci.

52. L. Vaganay, *An Introduction to the Textual Criticism of the New Testament*, 1937, p. 25.

53. The selections occur mainly in chapter 12 of Book III.

INDEX

Abraham, 102, 103, 105
Achaia, 42, 43, 58, 87, 116
Adriatic Sea, 61
Aeneas of Lydda, 89
Aesculapius (Asclepius), 9, 95
Agrippa, 69, *and see under* Herod
Akeldama (Field of Blood), 35, 95
Alexander of Ephesus, 13, 89, 94; of Abonuteichos, 95; high priest, 97
Alexandria, 12, 20, 60, 71, 80, 87, 88, 92, 93, 116, 121, 146
Amman, (*see* Philadelphia)
Ammonius of Alexandria, 159
Amphipolis, 60
Ananias, 97, 98, 119
Andocides, 25
Andrew, 89
Antioch, (Syrian), 12, 13, 61, 73, 87, 89, 132, 155; (Pisidian) 21, 43, 62, 75
Antipater, 75, 81
Antipatris, 64, 65
Antonia, 65
Antony, Mark, 65, 74, 75–76
Apamea, 73
Apollo, 48, 95
Apollonia, 60
Apollos, 28, 87, 89, 125, 155
apostles (the Twelve) 132, 143
Appian Way, 60, 61
Aquila, 28, 69, 87, 89, 94, 125, 126, 155
Arabia, 19–20, 127
Aramaic, 19, 33, 35, 67, 90, 98, 100, 104, 152
Aratus, 39, 46, 48, 49
Areopagus, 44, 51–52, 53
Aretas, 19–20
Aristarchus, 40, 89, 124, 125, 148
Aristeas, 48
army, Roman, 74, 79
Artemis, 5, 13, 41, 94
Asia, 40, 42, 63, 72, 87, 89, 121
Asiarchs, 42, 43, 82, 94
Assos, 61
Athenaeus, 21

Athens, 36, 43, 44–53, 86, 98, 160
Atonement, day of, 101
Atticists, 39
Augustan cohort, 59, 154
Augustan History, 71
Augustine, 18, 82
Augustus, 17, 18, 21, 28, 59, 62, 69, 75, 76, 81

Babylon, 104
Bacon, B. W., 130
Balogh, J., 18
barbarian, 11, 23, 25, 26, 32, 82
Bar-Jesus, 24, 97, 155
Barnabas, 21, 24, 28, 89, 97, 125, 127; Epistle of, 158
Barsabbas, 97–98, 118–119, 155
Bartholomew, 97
Batanea, 59
Beatty, Sir A. C., 114, 143
Beautiful Gate, 96
Benjamin, 89, 90, 125
Berea, 40, 43, 61
Bernice, 43, 97
Beth-horon, 64–65
Bethlehem, 63
bilingualism, 15, 21, 24, 33, 67
Billerbeck, Paul, 95
Bion of Soli, 17
birth certificate, 71–72
Bithynia, 14, 110, 121
Black Sea, 37, 91
Bostra, 64
Boswell, James, 133
Britain, 10
Brundisium, 61

Caesar, C. Julius, 44, 69, 74, 75, 76
Caesar, appeal to, 69, 78
Caesarea, 64, 132
Caligula, 20, 69
Callimachus, 47, 49
Candace, 15–18
Cappadocia, 121
Castor and Pollux, 60
Catholic Epistles, 144
census, 72–73, 76–77

Date Due